YOUNG RIDER'S HANDBOOK
HORSE CARE AND FITNESS
JO BIRD

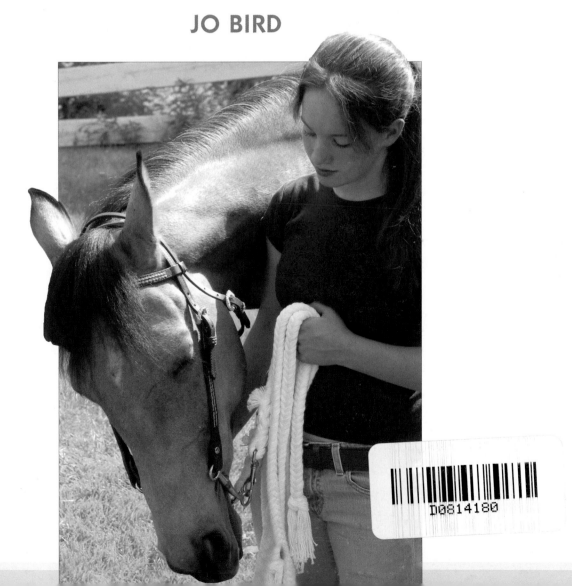

HORSE CARE AND FITNESS

JO BIRD

Credits

T.F.H. Publications
President/CEO: Glen S. Axelrod
Executive Vice President: Mark E. Johnson
Publisher: Christopher T. Reggio
Production Manager: Kathy Bontz
US Editor: Mary E. Grangeia
Cover Design: Mary Ann Kahn

T.F.H. Publications, Inc.
One TFH Plaza
Third and Union Avenues
Neptune City, NJ 07753

ISBN 978-0-7938-3202-6

Printed and Bound in China
08 09 10 11 12 1 3 5 7 9 8 6 4 2

Library of Congress Cataloging-in-Publication Data
Bird, Jo.
  Horse care and fitness / Jo Bird.
    p. cm.
  Includes index.
  ISBN 978-0-7938-3202-6 (alk. paper)
  1. Horses. I. Title.
  SF285.3.B57 2008
  636.1'083--dc22
                                    2007049529

The Leader In Responsible Animal Care For Over 50 Years!®
www.tfh.com

CENTRAL
Garden & Pet

Jo Bird

Jo Bird has owned horses for most of her life and used to juggle working as a groom in the mornings and going to an office job in the afternoons. She now provides management and nutritional advice to people buying horses and has worked in an advisory capacity helping to develop new products for a leading equestrian product manufacturer. She has owned a variety of horses, from foals to aged veterans and from huge, heavy traditional cobs to fine, fit racehorses. Her natural horsemanship philosophy is: "Think about it from the horse's point of view." She is the author of *Keeping a Horse the Natural Way* and *Breaking Bad Habits in Horses*.

Acknowledgments

Thanks to everyone at Sworders and to Lucy Back, Michelle Cogger, Ellen Cutlip, Katy Griffiths, Sarah Howe, Jo Jones, Laura Key, Gill Leage, Sarah Pamment, Adele Rawlinson and Gill Walker for allowing photoshoots. Thank you to my brilliant models: Charlotte Ellis, Kate and Lucy Fallen, Harriet de Freitas, Jeanette and Kelly Holzinger, Abbey and Leah Jolliffe, Jeannie Mott, Lotte Notley, Mary-Anne Reilly, Amber Tuckor and Alice Watts.

Contents

UNDERSTANDING HORSES

How does a horse's mind work? What is important to him? To build a good partnership with a horse, it helps to look at things from his point of view and to try to understand what is going on inside his head at any point in the day. Horses do not react to events in the same way as we humans do, and we have to recognize this when we take on the responsibility of looking after them.

COMPANY

Horses are herd animals by nature and therefore feel much more settled when they are in a group. You may have seen how some horses get very distressed if they are left in the field alone, or how some will "nap" (refuse to go forward when asked to do so) in order to get back home or to return to the other horses in a group lesson.

In the wild, a herd would be made up of mares, stallions, colts, and fillies of different ages, most of whom would be related. Most domestic male horses are castrated (gelded) to enable them to live in the groups we select for them without fighting with the other males or creating unwanted foals by mating with the fillies.

Within the group, there is a hierarchy whereby the most dominant horses influence the more subservient ones. This is not always achieved by a display of obvious aggression – you have probably seen horses back away from others who have just swished their tails or flattened their ears in a threatening gesture.

▲ **Take time to understand** *how your horse's mind "ticks." It will help your friendship to grow stronger.*

▼ **In the herd,** *the most dominant members eat first.*

◄ **A horse that is relaxed** *and contented will often be seen resting with a droopy lower lip, like this.*

▶ **Horses have very expressive ears** – *we can often learn a lot about their moods by getting to know what the "language of their ears" means.*

I'm alert and friendly

◀ **The flattened ears and purposeful stride** *say it all – this horse is unhappy with something and is warning others to back off and give him some space.*

I'm relaxed

◀ **Play fighting is usually** *an expression of high spirits rather than one of serious confrontation.*

I'm attentive

I'm angry

▲ **Horses are herd animals.** *In the wild, they live in a group that is led by the most dominant member of the herd.*

I'm afraid

I'm in pain or unhappy

Food and safety

In a domestic environment, horses rely on humans to provide food and shelter. In the wild, they cover many miles each day, grazing on the different types of vegetation that they come across and seeking out rivers or watering holes from which to drink. The most dominant horses will get to food or water first. In a domestic situation, you may see some horses getting bad-tempered if others come too close when they are feeding.

In bad weather, with or without the protection of blankets, horses tend to huddle in a line and "put their backs to the wind" because once they get cold or wet they have to use more energy just to keep warm. Eating plenty of forage, such as hay, actually generates heat within their bodies; however, if food is scarce, they risk losing weight in cold temperatures.

Even when a herd of horses sleep, some may sleep standing up (their legs can lock, which allows them to sleep standing upright without toppling over). Or several may lie down leaving at least one horse in the group standing on alert to any sign of danger.

What is important to us?
What generally makes people happy is seeing a smartly turned out, clean horse in shining tack and/or wearing the latest brightly colored blanket.

What is important to a horse?
Horses need companionship, adequate food and water and the freedom to roll in the dust or mud.

◀ **A particularly pungent odor** *can make a horse curl his lip, like this, to trap the smell deep in his nasal passages.*

◀ **Horses get a lot of water** *from moisture in growing plants; but in hot weather, they will not want to stray too far from their water source.*

▶ **Freedom to exercise** *without any constraints will enhance a horse's well-being and fitness. Let him have fun!*

▼ **We like to see a nice clean horse,** *but horses love to roll in dirt. It makes them feel good, and it helps to relieve an itch or get rid of shedding hair.*

Freedom & Play 10%

Safety 30%

Company 30%

Food & Water 30%

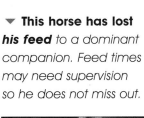

▼ **This horse has lost his feed** *to a dominant companion. Feed times may need supervision so he does not miss out.*

◀ **A horse's needs** *Understanding the basic things that are important to a horse will help us to make better sense of his actions when we take on the role of caregiver.*

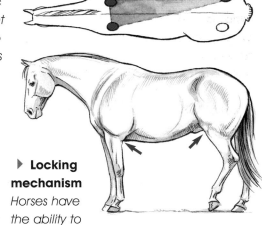

▶ **Locking mechanism** *Horses have the ability to lock the joints and ligaments in their elbows and stifles (the hindleg "knees") to enable them to sleep standing upright without falling over.*

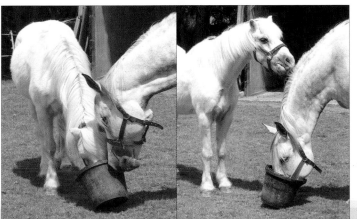

Getting to know your horse

Ears Horse have excellent hearing, far superior to our own. Each ear can move independently, enabling them to concentrate both on close sounds while still being aware of danger by detecting more distant signals. They sometimes bolt or spook at a noise that may be undetectable to us.

Eyes A horse's eyes are set on the side of his head. This gives him almost 360° all-around vision, the only blind spots being directly behind him and below the muzzle. While this is an excellent feature for detecting the approach of any predators, unfortunately it also means it is hard to creep up on a horse in order to slip a headcollar on him without being detected! Horses have good night vision, but their color spectrum is limited – this is not a problem in the wild, but it can cause confusion with depth of field when approaching colored poles in the show ring.

Muzzle The hairs on the muzzle are used as feelers to sense objects because horses cannot actually see this area. For this reason, it is best to leave them untrimmed on horses that live outdoors most of the time. They also have a highly acute sense of smell and can pick up the scent of other horses carried on the wind or by sniffing droppings left behind. Horses often display the Flehmen response to a strong or unusual fragrance. This is when a horse raises his head and curls back his top lip, which allows a special organ at the top of the nasal passage to assess an unfamiliar smell.

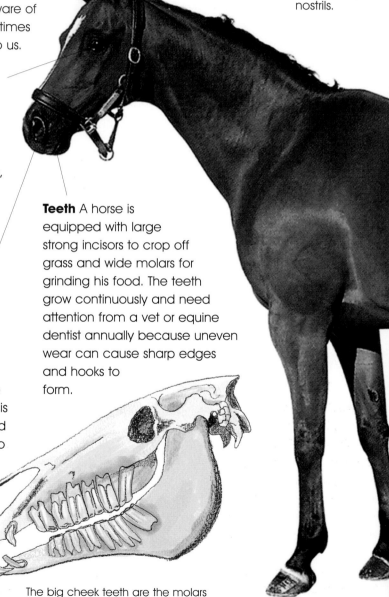

A relaxed horse will have a "soft" muzzle, ears, and nostrils.

Teeth A horse is equipped with large strong incisors to crop off grass and wide molars for grinding his food. The teeth grow continuously and need attention from a vet or equine dentist annually because uneven wear can cause sharp edges and hooks to form.

The big cheek teeth are the molars that grind up the horse's food.

TIP Get the vet to check your horse's teeth if he will not accept the bit or he drops his food. It is possible that sores in his mouth could be a problem.

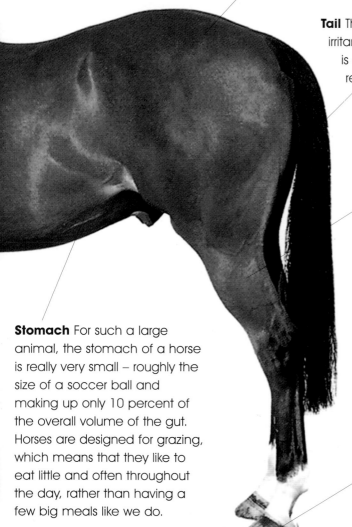

Skin/Hair A horse's coat grows thick in winter and sheds hair in summer. It is made up of hair follicles that stand up to trap air to keep him warm or flatten to dissipate heat when he needs to cool down. The skin is extremely sensitive to touch and is equipped with a twitch mechanism that enables the horse to move a small area of skin to dislodge a fly without the need to scratch it.

Tail The tail is immensely adept at swishing away flies and other irritants, and it also displays the mood of the horse in the way it is carried (e.g. high and taut = excited, low and loose = relaxed; taut and swishing = angry).

Legs The conformation of the legs (the way that they are formed and shaped) differs widely between different breeds of horse. Some have long, athletic limbs, with springy pasterns to cover the ground at high speed; some have thicker boned legs, with upright pasterns for a short, choppy stride; and others have a straight shoulder and a higher knee action good for driving.

Stomach For such a large animal, the stomach of a horse is really very small – roughly the size of a soccer ball and making up only 10 percent of the overall volume of the gut. Horses are designed for grazing, which means that they like to eat little and often throughout the day, rather than having a few big meals like we do.

Hooves The hooves have an outer layer of hard horn (a bit like the nails on our fingers) that surrounds the sensitive "layers" of the hoof wall, which actually bears the horse's weight. A shock-absorbing sole surrounds the frog (the rubbery V-shaped piece in the center of the foot), which helps to absorb the shock of impact as the foot hits the ground.

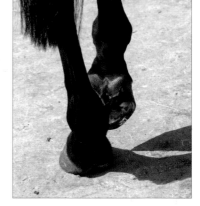

WHAT A HORSE NEEDS

SUITABLE GRAZING

The most natural way for horses to live is outdoors, where they are able to forage and roam freely in a herd environment. Although it is not always possible to offer total freedom all day long, it is essential for both their mental and physical well-being that they have access to grazing (or at least a turnout area with hay supplied) for a good portion of the day. Grass is nature's "super food," but horses also eat herbs, tree leaves, and bark for added vitamins and minerals.

- Grazing should ideally be able to supply much of the feed content that a horse or pony requires. For this reason, pastures should not be overgrazed by too many animals. Ideally, allow 1.5 acres (6000 sq m) per animal.
- Pastures and fields need to be well maintained and free of weeds.
  - The fields should be well drained so that they do not become boggy in winter.
    - Fencing should be safe and secure.

Remove: Poisonous plants such as ragwort, yew, laurel, privet, rhododendron, horsetail, and foxgloves can kill a horse or pony.

Control: Although weeds such as docks, nettles, and thistles do not harm horses, and certainly nettles and thistles have some beneficial feed value, do not let them encroach into your grass crop and take up valuable room that should be occupied by grass.

Keep compost separate: Grass cuttings ferment when left in a pile and can cause colic in horses and ponies if eaten. Never put cut flowers anywhere horses might reach them because many are poisonous to them.

▲ **Tailor your grazing** *to the needs of the types of horse that are on the land. Grass and herbage are the most natural diet for all equines.*

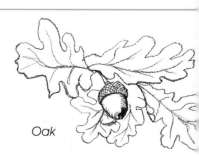

▶ **Know your plants.** *These are all poisonous to horses and should be eradicated from any areas that they may be able to reach.*

Oak

TIP It is best to divide a field into smaller paddocks so that grazed areas have time to rejuvenate. Think of grass as a crop – it has to be cared for in order to grow well.

Stable-kept horses

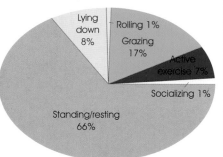

Lying down 8%
Rolling 1%
Grazing 17%
Active exercise 7%
Socializing 1%
Standing/resting 66%

Wild/naturally-kept horses

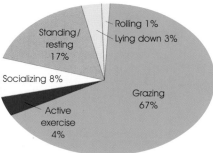

Standing/resting 17%
Rolling 1%
Lying down 3%
Socializing 8%
Active exercise 4%
Grazing 67%

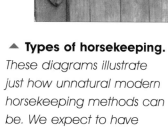

◄ **Eating wood and soil** may be symptoms of a mineral deficiency, so offer a mineral block or a comprehensive vitamin supplement.

▲ **Types of horsekeeping.** These diagrams illustrate just how unnatural modern horsekeeping methods can be. We expect to have athletic animals, yet horses stabled overnight can be almost immobile for about two-thirds of the day, instead of being active grazing outdoors during that time.

▲ **A stabled horse will relish a treat** of fresh grass and wild-picked herbs as a welcome change from his usual dry diet of hay and concentrates.

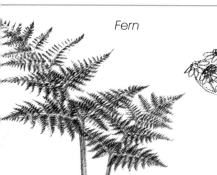
Fern

Ragwort

Rhododendron

Yew

Ivy

Outdoor shelter and water

SUITABLE SHELTER

Shelter is needed in a field so that horses can escape torment from flies and the hot sun, as well as to protect them in wet and windy weather. In the wild, horses would find shelter behind a large tree or hedgerow, so you should either provide the same natural features or a man-made shelter for any horses or ponies that are in your care. Structures should be sited facing away from prevailing winds. If a shelter or barn is to be shared by several horses or ponies, make sure any open sides are wide enough to accommodate several at once. This allows them to leave the shelter easily and can prevent accidents caused by squabbling.

WATER

The water content of grass can be as high as 80 percent but, as this varies tremendously according to the season, horses must always have access to clean water to slake their thirsts. Haylage (semi-wilted grass) contains between 35 to 50 percent water; this is significantly higher than hay, which is very dry and contains on average only 15 percent. This explains why some horses prefer it soaked or why they may even dip each mouthful in their water bucket! It can be dangerous if horses become dehydrated, and hard work or hot weather will mean that their water intake will increase. A hard-working horse or pony can lose up to 4.5 gallons (20 liters) of sweat in a day. An average of 5.5 to 15 gallons (25 to 70 liters) of water derived both from fluid and food will be needed per day. Water is necessary to help food pass through the gut, which can make a thirsty horse stop eating after awhile.

Water can be supplied by piping it to a trough (or an automatic waterer) or by filling buckets with a hose. A rainwater gutter and trough situated next to a field shelter is also a useful way to collect water in a remote place,

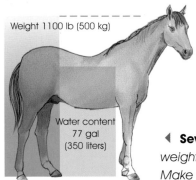

Weight 1100 lb (500 kg)

Water content 77 gal (350 liters)

▲ **Allow your horse access to fresh water** *at all times. In hot weather, his water intake will be greater than normal.*

◀ **Seventy percent** *of a horse's weight is made up of water. Make sure he gets plenty!*

▲ **Shelter from the sun** *is as important to horses as shelter from wind and rain.*

◀ **Often horses can sense a storm** *approaching and will get spooked. Make sure they have a shelter available.*

▶ **Site a field shelter** *so that the back bears the brunt of any bad weather. Allow room for the horses to be able to walk around it.*

Suitable stables

Whether you keep your horse at home or you board him, it is likely that you will need some kind of stabling even if he is kept out at grass most of the time. Stabling offers protection from extreme weather as well as a safe place to rest or recover from illness or injury. It also means that an owner can monitor the horse's food intake and condition while he is living in the stable area.

TRADITIONAL STABLES

Traditional stables are well-designed and safe. Internally, they should be at least 12 ft x 12 ft (3.6 m x 3.6 m) in size to give the horse or pony plenty of space in which to move and lie down. A courtyard design gives the occupants shelter from the elements plus a good view of the other horses. It is becoming increasingly popular to add windows to the back walls, too, to give the horse another view to enjoy and to improve air flow through the building.

▲ **A window on the world.**
Horses appreciate being able to see what is going on in the environment all around their stable.

INTERNAL BARN STABLING

A light, airy barn is divided up with rows of stables on each wall and a central corridor. Usually, the ceilings are high, which helps to maintain a pleasant temperature in both summer and winter. Often, internal stabling has grills between each stable that allow the horses to sniff and touch each other even when they are confined.

CORRALS

A concrete or sand/dirt area can be fenced off to confine your horse safely, while still allowing him some freedom and access to the outdoors when he chooses. There should be some shelter provided even if it is just a tarpaulin or roofed area he can walk underneath to avoid the full heat of the sun or a sudden downpour.

Remember: A horse would naturally walk 10 to 20 miles (16 to 32 km) a day in the wild so being confined to a stable is a very unnatural experience. Even stabling a horse overnight usually means that he will be stuck in the stable for about 15 hours at a stretch. Make sure that your horse has time out in the field or corral every day in addition to any ridden work that you do.

▲ **Stables that lead directly to turnout areas** *are very beneficial to your horse, particularly if he is able to move freely between the stable area and the pasture.*

▶ Stables should be palaces, not prisons! *This design combines features that will keep a horse or pony comfortable, safe, and secure.*

Lockable tack and feed room, with door wide enough for wheelbarrow

▼ Metal grills between stables *allow horses to maintain contact with neighbors.*

Security light

Exterior switches for lighting with waterproof cover

Opening skylight

Good ventilation

Security light

Muck heap

Good drainage

Rainwater collector

Concrete base with good drainage

Water tap and hose

Fire extinguisher

Stable cat for rodent control and company

Open window (at rear) to allow horse to put his head out

◀ This is an ideal setup *because the horses can leave the stables and enjoy the company of their stablemates in the fresh air outside when they choose to do so.*

17

Supervision and safety

SECURITY AGAINST THEFT

Horses and ponies are valuable, and it is unfortunately necessary to protect the animals we love from unscrupulous people who may want to steal them and sell them. Equipment, such as tack, blankets, and trailers, can also be at risk of theft, so to avoid the heartache of your property being stolen, follow the suggestions listed below:

- Keep all entrance gates to yards and fields closed and padlocked at all times.
- Have horses freeze-marked and/or microchipped, and display a sign stating that this has been done to act as a deterrent against would-be thieves.
- Visit the yard/field at different times of the day so that there are no long, regular periods of inactivity that a thief could take advantage of.
- Mark blankets with your postcode/zip code or the horse's freeze mark.
- If you are not yet old enough to drive, suggest to your parents or the adult who helps you to look after your horse that your postcode/zip code should be painted in large letters on the side and roof of your

trailer so that it can easily be identified by a police car or helicopter if it is stolen. Or recommend that a tracking device be installed.
- Have your tack security-marked and make sure all valuable items are insured.

SENSIBLE PRECAUTIONS

Post a sign on the yard that lists up-to-date telephone numbers of police, fire, and ambulance services, plus those of vets, farriers, and local friends who can help out in an emergency.

Once a week take a walk around all the fields and check the fencing for gaps or breakages. Pick up any litter (e.g. bottles, bags etc.) that may have been dumped or blown onto the land.

Check all woodwork in the stable yard for loose nails or splinters, which could injure a horse badly. Check metalwork, such as door cappings, hay racks, and hinges. Bent or rusty metal can have sharp edges and catch on blankets or cause injuries.

If you are short on time, try to come to make arrangements with someone to check on your horse for you. A blanket that has come unfastened and slipped down, or a sudden bout of colic, could have disastrous consequences if not discovered quickly. Never assume that you do not need to check your horse every day – horses are very accident-prone!

TIP A combination lock is useful; vets, farriers, and friends can be told the code, so you won't need to get lots of separate keys cut.

◀ **Sagging barbed wire** *can cause catastrophic injuries to horses.*

◀◀ **Solid posts and rails** *provide attractive, safe fencing, but check for splits or splinters in the wood.*

▼ **Walk around the fields and pastures** *weekly and check for hazards, such as holes and rubbish.*

◀ **Security and supervision** *are important day and night. Check locks before leaving.*

◀◀ **Having your horse freeze-marked** *is a good deterrent against theft.*

19

Blankets

A horse is very well equipped to cope with most weather conditions. His coat can shed or lie flat to keep him cool in hot weather and grow dense and fluff out to trap a warming layer of air to keep him comforable in the winter. However, there are still times when using a blanket will help to keep him in top condition.

DO use a blanket:
- If your horse is obviously cold or shivering.
- If your horse is outside during prolonged wet periods (to prevent a chill or rain scald).
- If your horse is underweight (to help him utilize the food he eats for weight gain and physical energy rather than just to keep warm).
- If the air temperature is cold and a stabled horse will be standing still for long periods or in a draughty or windy environment.
- In hot weather, when a horse may need a thin blanket or sheet to protect him from midge bites or to keep his coat cool or to avoid bleaching from the sun.

DO NOT use a blanket:
- If your horse or pony is too fat – let him use some of his feed intake to produce body heat naturally.
- If you are unable to check your horse regularly. With a blanket on he is unable to regulate his temperature. The weather can change suddenly, and it is up to you to add or remove blankets to keep him comfortable.
- If the blanket does not fit properly. Poorly fitting blankets can slip backwards and chafe the skin, and loose straps can catch on objects or get caught up in a horse's legs as he moves or struggles to get up.

▶ **A lightweight mesh fly sheet** *will stop irritation from biting midges and can also help to prevent sweet itch.*

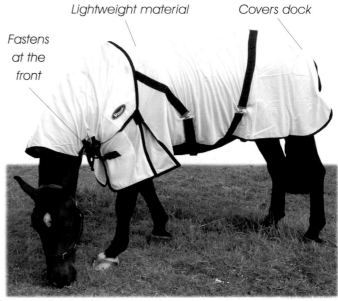

Lightweight material   *Covers dock*

Fastens at the front

TIP When fastening chest straps, bear in mind that your horse will want to put his head down to eat, so you may need to loosen the higher strap to keep it from digging in.

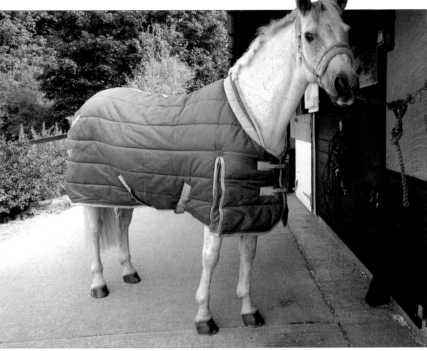

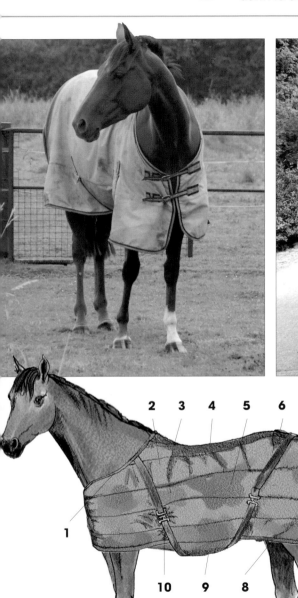

Points of a blanket

1 Correct size of neck aperture for proper fit.
2 Shoulder pleats here allow freer movement.
3 Proper coverage is from the top of the withers to the dock.
4 Darts and shaping along the back improve fit.
5 Breathable material wicks away moisture.
6 Avoid a seam on the back where dampness can seep through.
7 Tail guards reduce draughts and rubbing.

▲ **Be ready for all types of weather.** *Your kit should comprise both light and heavyweight turnout blankets and at least one stable blanket (shown above).*

8 Avoid leg straps because they can rub.
9 Length must stop draughts and cover the horse adequatley when lying down.
10 Adjustable, secure fastenings are a must.

How to put on and remove a blanket

PUTTING ON A BLANKET

1. Fold the back and front halves of the blanket inward until you are left with a panel not much wider than a saddlecloth. It will be easier to carry and lift over the horse and less likely to flap and startle him.
2. Unfurl the front section ensuring that the hair remains flat underneath. Fasten the chest buckles first, and allow plenty of room for your horse to put his head down when he grazes.
3. Work backwards and open out the blanket carefully.
4. Pull the tail through the tail loop. Fasten any leg straps. They should loop through each other to avoid chafing and be positioned so they do not catch when the horse lies down.
5. Fasten the belly straps in a diagonal pattern – left strap across to right buckle, right strap into left buckle. Allow slack of about a palm's width under the belly.
6. A well-fitting blanket should not rub or slip backwards.

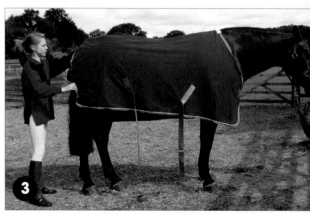

Well-fitting blanket

Blanket rubbing on withers

Leg straps too loose

Blanket too large

◀ **It is not only the length** *and depth of a blanket that is important. For a good fit, the neck aperture needs to be right or it will rub bare patches on the shoulders or slip back and rub the withers.*

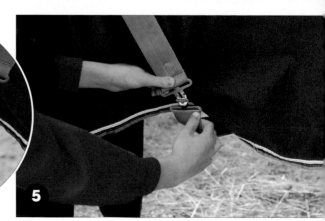

TIP If you have a dark-colored horse, a white cotton summer sheet can be used to reflect the sun. This limits bleaching of the coat and keeps him cooler.

REMOVING A BLANKET

Undo the straps from back to front – first leg straps, then belly straps, and finally the chest straps (**1**). This is just in case your horse should get loose while you are removing the blanket – if the chest straps were undone first, the blanket might slip back and get tangled around his hind legs with catastrophic consequences. (**2**) Either fold the blanket inward to make it easier to lift off, or grasp it at the withers and rump and slide it off backwards so that the straps do not knock against your horse.

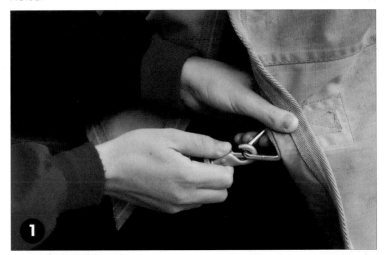

Keeping your horse up-to-date

In addition to daily care and attention, a responsible horse owner will keep up-to-date on the following health, legal, and travel matters.

PASSPORT

When you purchase a horse, he may come with various documents and even a passport for travel abroad (mandatory in the UK). These often include details of the specific breeding and exact date of birth if known, or may be more general with just a description of the horse's identification markings, which have been endorsed by a vet. These include color, position of whirls (where the hair swirls against the lie of the coat), and any freeze mark, brand, or identification chip the horse may have.

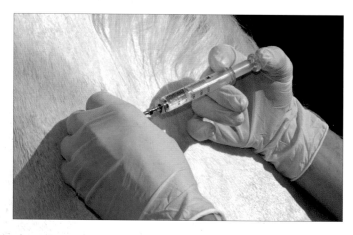

INSURANCE

Insurance coverage should include, at a minimum, third-party claims (for example, if your horse kicks another and injures him or damages property like a stable or trailer), and also vet's fees caused by illness or injury. A long-term illness, fracture of a bone, or an attack of colic that requires an operation could easily run up fees of several thousand dollars. Without adequate insurance coverage, it may not be financially possible to save your animal.

DEWORMING

Most animals naturally carry some form of internal parasites from time to time, but a heavy worm burden can have serious health consequences for a horse or pony, including weight loss, anaemia and colic. Good pasture management, including clearing droppings and field rotation, helps with assistance from a carefully planned use of chemical dewormer, chosen according to the season and specific worm eggs and larvae you are treating. A small sample of manure can be sent to a laboratory to assess if there is a parasite problem.

VACCINATIONS

Vaccinations are usually recorded on the horse's papers, and it is often a requirement to show proof of up-to-date health records when traveling abroad or competing. Protection against equine influenza (flu) and tetanus are usually essential, while vaccination against equine herpes is a requirement in some racing and stud yards, with additional protection being needed if required by state or international laws.

TIP Ask your vet to send you a reminder when your horse is due for his annual vaccinations or dental check so that you do not forget.

DENTAL CARE

Having good teeth is an essential part of survival for a horse. Problems such as jaw abscesses or missing or sharp teeth will severely affect their ability to chew fibrous forage and grains, which will result in possible impaction colic (a digestive problem in which food stops moving along the animal's bowel) or poor nutrient absorption. A dental check by a vet or equine dentist once or twice a year will eliminate discomfort caused by sharp hooks or infected teeth. Horses are usually better patients than we are in the dentist's chair!

bare and simply have them trimmed and shaped by a farrier every couple of months. Many horses and ponies can be worked very successfully in this way. If you wish to try your horse unshod when he has previously worn shoes, bear in mind that the transition will take at least three months. Also, during this time he will have very sensitive feet before they harden up – ouch!

If you ride on very abrasive ground or predominantly on roads, shoeing may be more appropriate. Shoes can be fitted (with the addition of road nails or studs if required), which will prevent the hooves from wearing too quickly and causing sores or bruises. Bear in mind that you will be tied to a six- to eight-week cycle of farrier visits to trim off the excess hoof, which is still growing above the shoe. Overgrown feet can put strain on the joints and raised clenches (nails) can cause splits in the hoof wall. If your horse loses a shoe as a result, it means you won't be able to ride!

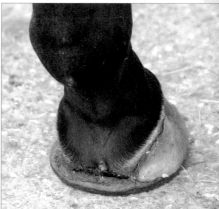

HOOF CARE

Horses hooves grow approximately ⅜ in (1 cm) per month. In the wild, hooves would wear down naturally as horses roamed around the rough ground of their pastures. It is quite possible to keep hooves naturally

▲ **Farriers have good knowledge** *of anatomy and will help keep your horse sound whether he is shod or unshod.*

▲ **Remedial shoeing** *can help with faults. This eggbar shoe can help support a collapsed heel or navicular bone.*

REGULAR ROUTINES

DAILY CHECKLIST FOR A FIELD-KEPT HORSE

- Visit your horse at least twice a day. It would be dreadful to find him caught up in his blanket or injured and know that he may have been in distress for a long time before his plight was discovered.

- Take time to check if your horse is grazing calmly or standing looking anxious or uncomfortable. If he is standing awkwardly and is reluctant to move, he may have succumbed to an inflammation of the tissues of the hoof called laminitis (see pages 88-89 for more details). If he is rolling and sweating or rolling incessantly (*above*), he could be suffering from abdominal pain caused by colic.

SUMMER ISSUES

- Approach your horse and run your hand over his body to check for bumps, bites, or scratches that you may not notice from a distance. It is a good idea to feel for excessive heat in the hooves and to pick out the feet to remove stones that could cause bruising.

- Some horses wear mesh blankets in the summer to protect them from biting midges, or a light-colored blanket to stop the sun from overheating them and bleaching the coat.
- Apply a fly repellent/fly fringe if necessary.
- Clean and refill water troughs or containers if they are green with algae or contaminated with food or bird droppings. Stale water is not palatable.
- Pick up droppings in the field, unless you have a large field that can be chain-harrowed by a tractor. Droppings can be removed either by hand or nowadays by vacuum-type towable collectors to make cleaning the fields easier. Fields can be harrowed provided they can be rested afterwards. This needs to be done in hot weather to kill off any worm larvae in the droppings.
- If your horse or pony is putting on weight, he may need to have his grazing restricted by moving him to a corral or stable for part of each day/night.

TRY THIS: On a hot day, feel the contrast in skin temperature between a grey horse and a dark bay or black horse. Or on a colored or paint horse, feel the temperature difference between the dark and light patches.

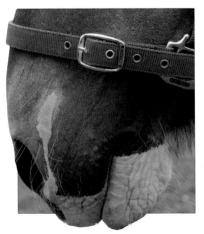

◀ **In summer, it is essential to protect pink muzzles** *with sunscreen or they will blister. Apply it daily because it rubs off easily.*

▼ **This mesh fly mask** *totally prevents flies from irritating a horse's eyes and ears.*

▲ **A fly fringe** *works like an extension of your horse's forelock to help flick the flies away.*

◄ **Raking up droppings daily** *will keep the pasture fresh and reduce the likelihood of flies and worms affecting your horse's health.*

◄◄ **Provide more than enough water** *to last until your next visit to the field.*

27

Daily routines

WINTER ISSUES

- Feel if your horse is warm enough and put a blanket on him if he is losing condition just trying to stay warm. Put on a dry blanket if the one he is wearing is soaked through.
- Feed hay if grass is poor, and supplement the diet with cereals (see pages 56-57) if he is working hard or requires more condition.
- It is a good idea to add tepid water to any feed – some horses resist drinking icy water and may suffer impacted colic if the feed is dry.
- Break any ice that has formed on the water trough.
- Check fencing because it can become damaged by high winds or falling branches.
- Even if you are not riding your horse, examine him thoroughly (although do not groom him too regularly – he needs the natural grease in his coat to stay warm in the cold weather).

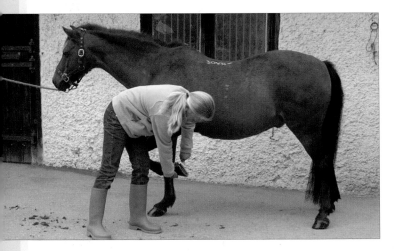

- Hose off mud on the legs and pick out the feet every couple of days (*above*). You may not otherwise see if he is suffering from mud fever or thrush (see pages 88-91) if he is coated in mud.

Note: Horses and ponies can survive very cold temperatures, but have more trouble coping with long periods of rain. They can catch a chill and become very miserable, and being wet can cause "rain scald," which makes their hair scabby and fall out in "clumps!" *Keep him warm and dry.*

**DAILY CHECKLIST FOR
A STABLED/PART-STABLED HORSE**

- Morning feed (possibly prepared the night before).
- Depending on the season, change the blanket.
- Examine the horse; check for filled (puffy) legs.
- Groom and ride or put on a headcollar and lead your horse out to the turnout area or pasture.
- Muck out the stable and prepare for the evening.
- Empty, clean, and refill water buckets.
- Fill up hay nets and hang up ready for the evening (or soak for 10 minutes then leave out to drain).
- Allow your horse as much time out as possible, then fetch him in from the field.
- Tie him up outside and pick out his feet.
- Remove any outdoor blankets and check him over for wounds; brush and reblanket if necessary.
- Put your horse to bed in his stable.
- Prepare feed for the next day.

Remember: Horses do not sleep for eight hours or so during the night as we do. They take short naps of just 5 to 10 minutes (or longer if they choose to lie down) throughout the entire 24-hour period of a day. This stems from their inborn instinct to be ready to flee from danger at any time. You can understand how some horses can get bored when they are stuck in a confined space for long periods.

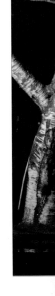

TIP Provide field-kept horses with big bales of hay and large water troughs. This way they can self-feed and will not go without if, for some reason, you are late.

◀ **Horses are very good at keeping warm,** *even in the snow. Wet weather is more of a problem to them.*

You can get a good idea if your horse is warm by feeling the temperature around the base of his ear or behind his elbow.

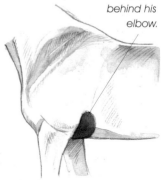

Even with a blanket on, you can feel these areas. A sweaty or shivering horse will not be comfortable.

◀ **After hosing,** *dry the legs with a towel before turning out or stabling.*

◀◀ **Nights are long** *for a stabled horse – top off hay as late as you possibly can.*

29

Grooming

FULL GROOMING

If you watch horses reacting to one another in the field, you'll notice that they groom their friends by nibbling them with their teeth. So when you give your horse a thorough grooming session, you will make him adore you! Imagine the itchiness they must feel when their coat is shedding in clumps or the irritation they feel when being bitten by midges – wouldn't it be such a relief to have your entire body brushed if you were in their position?

1. Tie up your horse and remove any blankets.
2. Start at the neck area and using a body brush (or dandy brush if the coat is very long) use long, firm, sweeping strokes following the lie of the coat. Regularly remove hair from the brush with a curry comb.
3. Use a rubber curry comb in a circular motion to remove clumps of mud or matted hair. Only use a body brush on the face and legs as these bony areas are very sensitive and can be easily bruised.
4. Using separate damp sponges, wipe around the eyes, the nostrils and muzzle, the teat area in a mare and the sheath area of a gelding, and under the dock.
5. Mist the mane with some detangling spray, and comb it all onto the other side of the neck, then brush it back over in small sections to remove any knots. If you find that there are stray hairs that insist on sticking up, either dampen them or use human hair gel to set them in place.
6. Coat the tail with detangling spray and, working on a small section at a time, tease out the knots with your fingers so that the brush will pass through the tail hairs easily. You may have to hold the hairs across your knee to be able to brush the ends of them effectively.

7. Scrape off any mud from the outside of the hooves and pick out the inside of each hoof. Using a brush dipped in water, scrub off any mud residue from the outside of the hooves.
8. Dip a small towel in clean water, wring it out to be almost dry, and then wipe it over the horse's entire body; this will lift the dust (inset detail) and lay the hair flat.
9. Finish by applying a mist of show sheen spray. Remember not to put it on the saddle area or you risk a disaster when your saddle starts slipping! After the hooves have dried, a coat of hoof oil provides the finishing touch.

Color code your sponges *for different purposes, or mark them with a permanent marker so you always use the same one on the same area of the body.*

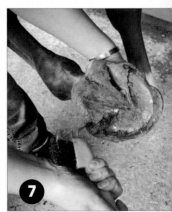

TIP Keep a pack of baby wipes (fragrance-free) in your grooming kit. They are a handy way to clean the eyes, nose, and dock instead of using damp sponges.

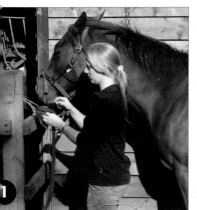

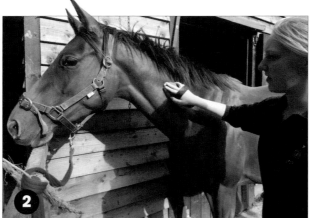

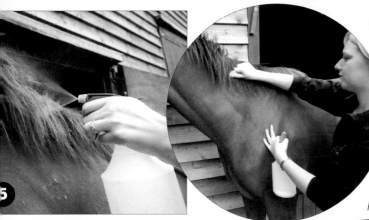

If your horse has not had a thorough makeover for a while, his tail may have grown too long. Trim it square at the bottom, roughly 4 in (10 cm) below the level of the hock. Show sheen applied to the tail every time you groom will help prevent the hair from breaking and knotting. If your horse has long feathers on his legs, apply the spray here too and work it through with your fingers to repel water and mud. Chalk powder or whitener sprays can be used to neutralize staining and brighten white hairs.

Grooming

A QUICK GROOM

If you have limited time before riding, or your horse is living out in the field and excessive grooming is not advisable (you do not want to strip the oils from his coat), then a quick check over and groom is sufficient. He may not look gleaming, but he should be comfortable enough to be ridden.

1. Tie up your horse and remove any blankets.
2. Concentrate on the areas where the tack will go because mud in these areas would chafe and make him sore. Remove any dried mud from the head with a soft brush or your fingers. If the mud is wet, use a damp sponge, and then dry the area with a towel.
3. Brush away any mud from the saddle area and particularly the area under his tummy where the girth will lie, just behind the elbow.
4. Pick out his feet.

PROTECTION AIDS

On a day-to-day basis, it is unlikely that your horse will need to wear any boots or bandages. For more demanding outings, such as jumping or cross-country events where he may be likely to take a knock or his legs will come under additional strain, they can be a useful addition to your basic tack.

When you first pick them up, often it is hard to work out whether a boot is for the foreleg or the hind leg. Usually, boots designed to go on the hind legs will be longer and may have more fixing straps. The straps should always be fastened on the outside of the leg, with the ends facing backwards.

Did you know?

- Overreaching is when a horse's hind legs travel too far forward and catch the heel of the foreleg, sometimes causing a cut.

▲ **Your horse may want to groom you too;** *it's only natural, but sometimes it may hurt – ouch!*

◀ **Poor conformation** *can cause a crooked action like brushing, which may result in knocks to the legs.*

Stepping out too far ▶ *with a hind leg can cause an overreach injury to the foreleg.*

TIP It is faster and safer to use modern boots fixed with velcro straps for riding than attempting to bandage legs with cotton or fleece bandages, which require special skill to fasten correctly.

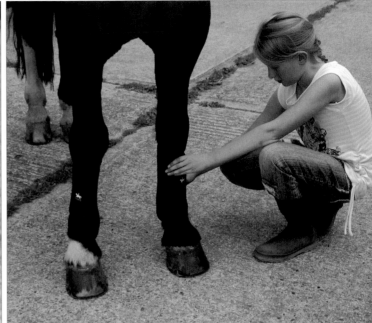

▲ **With brushing boots,** the strike pad should face the inside. They should be positioned below the knee and just cover the inside of the fetlock.

Wrap the boots tightly so they will not slip down, and fasten the fixings securely, with the straps on the outside and facing backwards.

◀ **Overreach boots protect** the horse from injury should he step on himself with the opposite foreleg or hind leg.

▶ **The value of protective boots** can be seen in action as this athletic animal takes a fence.

Hoof care

Hoof care is vitally important because without healthy hooves your horse may easily go lame. The farrier is as important as a vet because he will examine and rebalance the hooves by trimming and shoeing them correctly. However, you need to practice general health care as well. Something as simple as a small crack or a trapped stone could make your horse unridable for several weeks if left to deteriorate. Common problems include bruised soles, cracks and chips in the hoof, abscesses, and thrush infections.

1. Tie up your horse with a quick-release knot.
2. Keep a shallow rubber bucket or feed bowl reserved for the job. You will use it to catch the dirt that you clean out of the hoof, and it will save you time sweeping up afterwards.
3. Stand parallel to your horse, facing his tail. Bend down or squat so you can easily move away if he should kick out.
4. Run your hand down the back of his leg and lift the hoof from the fetlock. If he resists, lean against the shoulder (foreleg) or quarters (hind leg) of the leg you are cleaning; this will shift his weight away from this leg and make it lighter to lift.
5. Lift his leg up, and cup the hoof in the palm of your hand.
6. Tuck the hoof pick into the top corners on either side of the frog (just behind where the shoe finishes). The frog is the V-shaped fleshy part that extends out from the heel.
7. Using a heel-to-toe motion, scrape out mud, trapped bedding, or stones, being careful not to prick the sensitive frog.
8. Some hoof picks have a brush attached, which is useful in clearing away fine debris and dust.
9. When the hoof is clean, slowly and gently lower it to the ground and move on to the next hoof.

Warning: Some horses are reluctant to lift their hind legs very high as this unbalances them, so they may kick out in protest. Be gentle and keep the leg low enough to be comfortable for them. Always be cautious when working around the hindquarters of a horse; you can be badly hurt if a horse kicks out suddenly and catches you with his hoof.

There are various hoof products available on the market that do different things. Hoof hardeners will toughen the hoof wall and sole and are useful for barefoot horses or those with hooves that have been weakened by frequent nail holes. Hoof oils serve mainly to enhance the appearance of a healthy hoof. Hoof moisteners assist in nourishing and maintaining moisture within the hoof to try to prevent cracking.

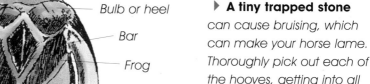

▶ **Learn the points of the hoof** *so that you will understand advice your farrier may give you.*

White line
(junction between
horn and sole)

Wall (horn)

Bulb or heel

Bar

Frog

Collateral
groove

Point of frog

Sole

▶ **A tiny trapped stone** *can cause bruising, which can make your horse lame. Thoroughly pick out each of the hooves, getting into all the crevices and corners to remove any grit. Hooves impacted with mud or wet bedding risk contracting thrush (see page 90).*

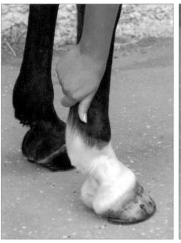 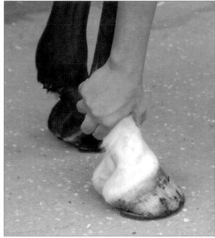 

▲ **To lift a horse's hoof,** *gently slide your hand down the tendons and lean into the horse to shift his weight over from the leg you want to raise.*

An obstinate horse will lift a hind leg if you squeeze the hock. Lift from the pastern or feathers, and support the weight with your hands.

▲ **Hoof hardener** *strengthens the structure of the hoof wall and sole in an unshod horse.*

▶ **Hoof oil** *adds a nice sheen for a polished appearance.*

Bathing

For tip-top presentation for a show or to freshen up a horse in hot weather, a bath can be beneficial. Some shampoos also benefit the horse by helping to repel flies or eliminate scurf as well.

Only consider bathing your horse if the weather is warm or he may catch a chill. In colder temperatures, treat any dirty areas with a stain-remover spray and just clean stains section by section by dabbing them with a damp sponge.

Some horses dislike water altogether and some have a fear of hoses; the shape may remind them of a snake hiding in the grass perhaps. For nervous horses, and in anything other than the hottest of weather, it is advisable to fill buckets with warm water so as not to alarm them and keep them comfortable.

1. It is easier to do one side of your horse at a time, and then do the other side to avoid him standing with a wet coat for too long a period. Dampen the coat, then massage in the shampoo, working it in well with your fingers – your horse will love this!

2. Work the shampoo through the hairs of the mane. Do the same with the tail, or lift the bucket up so that the tail dips into it. After shampooing it, swill it around to give it a thorough rinse.

3. With a water-laden sponge or a watering can, drench the shampooed coat, working from the back downwards to thoroughly cleanse the coat of the shampoo. A tolerant horse may allow you to use a hose to do this. Repeat until the water runs clear and no traces of soapy foam can be seen.

4. Using a rubber sweat scraper, work from neck to tail with long strokes, following the lie of the hair to remove excess water.

5. Stand to the side of your horse and hold the tail hairs just below the dock. Keeping the dock portion still, spin the lower hairs like a windmill to get excess water off the tail. Tell everyone else to get out of the way or they are likely to get soaked!

6. To finish, rub your horse over with a clean towel, paying particular attention to the base of his ears, his elbows, and legs and heels. Use a waffle-weave cooler or a sweat blanket (with a cotton blanket on top if the weather is cool) to allow the water to evaporate while avoiding the risk of the horse getting a chill.

TIP A horse's tail can be washed throughout the year to keep it clean and tangle-free. Your horse will not feel cold unless you soak the dock – then you will see him shudder!

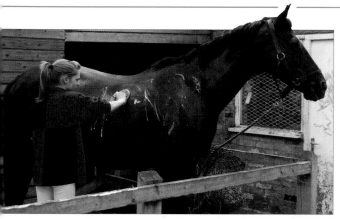

1 *Dampen the coat, then massage in the shampoo.*

2 *Rub shampoo into the mane and tail hairs also.*

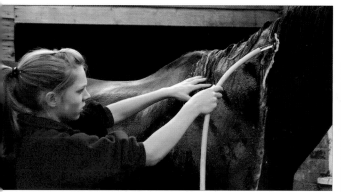

3 *Rinse the coat thoroughly to remove the soap suds.*

4 *Most of the water will be squeezed out with a sweat scraper.*

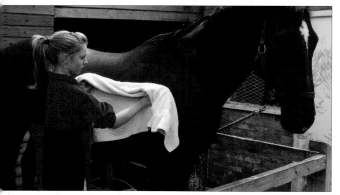

5 *Towel dry to prevent your horse from getting a chill.*

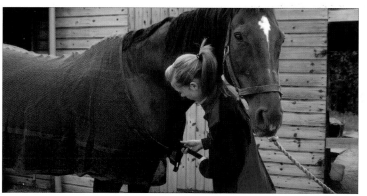

6 *Use a waffle-weave cooler blanket to wick away any moisture.*

Should I clip my horse ?

Horses naturally shed their coats in the spring and begin to grow a thick, dense coat in the autumn to keep them warm during the winter months. Many horses can manage without a blanket during the winter provided they can find shelter from prolonged rain.

The downside to having this thick coat is that when we ride or work them actively, they will soon get too warm and start to sweat. Sweat is uncomfortable for horses and it will make their coat sticky and difficult to groom, even when dry. If you only ride your horse a couple of times a week, it is probably better to put up with this than risk him getting cold or having to wear several blankets because you have clipped him. If you ride your horse regularly and the sweating is becoming a problem, then consider clipping him.

But which clip should you choose? Ideally, only take off the minimum of hair in the areas where he sweats – usually, the neck and girth area. Remember that your horse will have to wear a blanket if you take off some of his coat, unless the weather is very mild. A clip will usually last for about six weeks before it needs to be redone.

SUMMER CLIPPING

It is not usual to clip horses when spring is approaching because this may affect the summer coat that is coming through. Some horses do not lose their coats readily or they naturally have thick coats all year round, and in such cases it is kinder to clip them during the summer to keep them more comfortable.

HOGGING MANES

Some horses have their manes cut off (hogging). You will see polo ponies with hogged manes and also some heavy cob types. If a pony has sweet itch, it may be smarter and kinder to hog his mane rather than leave him to rub it until it ends up looking like a loo brush!

▲ **Neck and Chest Clip**
Useful for horses living out who sweat when ridden; most of the coat remains.

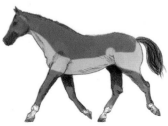

▲ **Trace Clip**
Ideal for working horses; it keeps them cool and makes grooming easier.

Warning: Do not hog a horse on a whim. It takes nearly a year for the mane to grow back fully, and in the in-between stages your horse's hair will stand up vertically like a "mohawk" haircut!

CLIPPING FEATHERS

Some native and heavy breeds grow long hairs around the coronet and pastern, and these feathers (as they are called) can stretch up as high as the back of the knee. Although stunning to look at, they need a lot of care and attention and can soak up wet and mud like a sponge, which makes them very heavy and difficult to dry out. You may want to cut off the feathers to prevent mites from burrowing in the long hairs, or simply to change your horse's appearance – from hairy heels to short and neat. So perfect your clipping skills!

Warning: Clipping involves sharp, fast-moving blades, and often electrical equipment. It should only be done by experienced people who can handle the horse and the equipment safely.

TIP To avoid nicks to wrinkly skin, ask a helper to stretch out each foreleg while you clip the elbows.

▲ **Chaser Clip**
Similar to the Trace Clip, but all or part of the head hair is clipped too.

▲ **Irish Clip or Low Trace**
Ideal for most working horses; only areas that sweat are clipped.

▲ **Blanket Clip**
Useful for working horses, and appealing for those with hogged manes.

▲ **Hunter Clip**
For stabled and hard-working horses. Leg hair is often left on for protection.

◄ **Some people choose to** remove whiskers from the muzzle. Horses use these as feelers, so it is kinder to keep these if possible.

▶ **Keep the mane tied** out of reach of the clippers. Remember that you cannot put back what's clipped off!

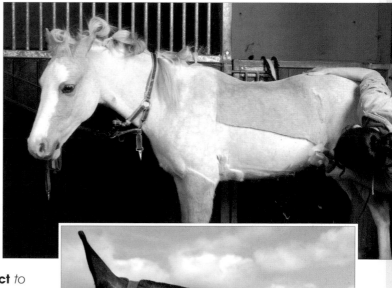

◄ **Many horses object** to having their ears clipped – it may tickle in a sensitive spot or sound like a buzzing fly.

▶ **On the right type of horse,** a newly hogged mane looks stunning.

Mucking out

The repetitive daily chore of cleaning the stable can be a dreaded task for many horse owners. If you do not have the benefit of extensive grazing or are bound by rules of a boading establishment, it is likely you will have to stable your horse for part of the day and/or night. And in that case you will be faced with the fact that you will have to muck out the stable on a regular basis.

From the horse's point of view, bedding has the following functions:

- It provides somewhere comfortable for him to lie down, preventing possible knocks and injury.
- It allows him to urinate without splashing his legs.
- It provides insulation and a draught-free environment.
- It enables him to dig around in the bedding material and carry out foraging activities, which a bare concrete floor would not allow.

TYPES OF BEDDING

Straw

A straw bed can look wonderfully inviting – even soft enough for us to sleep on! Wheat straw is cheap and readily available while barley straw makes the softest, golden-colored bed. The straw you use should be dry, nondusty and mold-free. Although it makes the cosiest of beds, straw is probably the hardest type of bedding to muck out and it creates the biggest muck heap to clean.

Note: Many horses will eat a straw bed and while normally it should do them no harm, a greedy horse could suffer colic or put on undesired extra weight by excessive consumption of straw.

Chopped Straw

As it sounds, this is composed of short strands of straw, supplied in plastic wrapped bales so they can be stored outside. Clean and easily biodegradable without creating a vast muck heap, it is an excellent choice for all but the wettest of horses.

Shavings

Wood shavings supplied in a plastic-wrapped bales give the cleanest appearance and tend to be the most absorbent type of bedding. They are more expensive, and the bales are heavy to handle.

Hempcore

Stems of the hemp plant are supplied in plastic-wrapped bales. It offers high absorbency in a shallower bed but can be harder to manage than shavings, and it is an unappealing dull grey/brown color.

TIP Take your horse out of the stable before mucking out because disturbing the bed will cause dust particles to be released into the air, which will not be good for his breathing.

▶ **Many horses learn to regard** *their stable as a place of safety in which they can rest. It is our responsibility to provide a comfortable, dry bed with forage to help them relax while they are confined indoors.*

Check that any bedding you buy is free of mold and dust.

▲ **There are many types of bedding** *on the market, so it is important that you weigh the pros and cons of each in relation to your budget and your horse's needs.*

Shredded Paper

Recycled paper can be put to good use. In fact, it is quite possible to shred your own newspaper, but you will need a mountain of papers and a production line of people to produce enough for a bed!

Rubber Matting

These compressed rubber sheets (*right*) have excellent insulation and shock-absorbing properties. They can be used on their own or covered with a thin layer of bedding that is banked up at the sides. After the initial cost outlay, rubber mats make a huge difference in terms of speed and ease of mucking out.

How to muck out

The tools you will need are:
- a wheelbarrow
- a shovel
- a fork (wide-pronged for dealing with straw and narrow-pronged for shavings)
- a stiff broom

1. Remove all feed and water buckets. You do not want them contaminated with dust and dirt while you are shaking and moving the bedding around.
2. Begin by lifting any obvious piles of droppings with your fork or shovel. Tip them into the wheelbarrow while trying to leave behind as much of the bedding as possible. Throw the clean bedding high onto the banks.
3. Pick up the droppings that are then exposed – use gloves to protect your hands and keep them clean if it is too difficult working with a fork.
4. Using the shovel, dig out the areas of wet bedding.
5. Sweep the center of the floor clean and, if you have time, leave it to dry out.
6. Fork down the clean bedding that you had thrown to the sides, and lay the floor of the bed. Unless you are using rubber mats, this should be around 6 to 12 in (15 to 30 cm) deep (depending on the type of bedding used). The floor should not be exposed by the horse's feet when he moves or lies down.
7. Add some fresh bedding on top if the bed is getting thin.
8. Rebuild the banks to protect the horse from draughts and to keep him away from the walls. Otherwise, you risk him getting cast (stuck) when he tries to get up. Finally, with the back of the fork, flatten the bed and shape the banks. What a tidy bed!

DEEP LITTER

A deep litter bed means that just the droppings and the worst of the wet bedding are removed without disturbing the main body of the bed. Fresh bedding is just added on top so that it is dry for the horse to lie down on. This is most useful if your horse is kept in a barn because the whole barn can just be dug out periodically by tractor.

Advantages:
- It takes a lot less time on a daily basis.
- A full muck out is only required every month or couple of months.
- It uses less bedding and is more economical.

Disadvantages:
- When the bed is eventually dug out, the bedding is heavy and it really smells.
- The air in the stable can become stale or smell unpleasantly of ammonia.
- If the bedding gets too wet, the horse will lie in this soiled material and he also risks contracting thrush in his hooves from the wet environment (see page 90).

TIP If you visit your horse late at night to feed him, take the opportunity to pick up any droppings so they won't get mixed into the bed overnight.

INTERIM CLEANING

To make stable cleaning an easier chore, just remove the droppings left on the surface of the bed until the next muck out. Use a shovel or fork to gather them up, or do what many people prefer to do and put on rubber gloves and scoop them into a bucket or basket.

▲ **For a quick cleanup,** *use rubber gloves and simply pick droppings up off the surface.*

▲ **For a more thorough cleanup,** *a wheelbarrow and fork are needed for all that wet muck!*

43

Cleaning tack

Apart from mucking out, one of the hardest jobs in horse care is cleaning tack. Tack soon gets greasy from the horse's sweat and, if left this way, it can rub causing sores on the skin. The leather itself will also suffer and may crack, go stiff, or develop mildew if left damp. Cleaning tack need not be a chore; it can be very rewarding – the end result is clean, shiny tack and, of course, your horse will look so sharp!

CLEANING YOUR SADDLE

1. Put your saddle on a saddle horse, or the arm of a chair, fence rail, or stable door.
2. Fill a bucket half-full of warm water, and add just a drop of detergent, which will help to dissolve grease.
3. Remove the girth, stirrup leathers, and irons from the saddle.
4. Take the irons off the leathers, and drop them in the bucket of water to soak.
5. Dip a sponge in the water and squeeze it out so it is damp (but not saturated). Wipe over the entire saddle, lifting up the saddle and girth flaps and not forgetting the underside.
6. Pay attention to greasy areas. Small spots of grease are referred to as "jockeys," and you may need to use your finger nail or a teaspoon to scrape them off. (Do not use a knife or you may scratch the leather.)
7. Now either apply liquid soap onto the tack or rub the tub or bar of saddle soap with your damp sponge and apply it to the leather.
8. You will notice how the leather shines after the soap is applied.
9. Clean and soap the stirrup leathers and refit the irons.
10. The finished job looks great!

Note: Girths made of material or webbing should have the hair and mud brushed off and be washed in the washing machine. You can pop a sock over the buckles at each end of the girth, or wash the girth inside a pillow case to protect the machine.

▲ **Cleaning tack** *can be rewarding. It is good to know your tack is safe, well cared for, and gleaming!*

7

TIP If you want the leather to look shiny, keep the sponge as dry as possible when applying the soap to prevent it from getting frothy and streaky. Think of it as a polish, rather than as a soap!

1

2

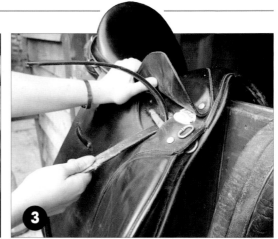

3

4

5

6

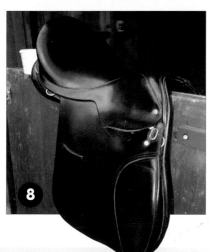

8

9

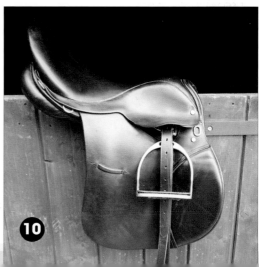

10

Cleaning the bridle

1. Find somewhere to hang your bridle – a coat hook will do.
2. Either take the bridle apart (warning: you must know how to put it back together again) or take all the straps out of their holders but keep the buckles done up.
3. Begin on one side and work your way down from the headpiece to the bit, wiping the leather with a sponge dipped in water and detergent.
4. Work your way down each side, removing any grease and mud. Clean the reins thoroughly too.
5. When you reach each buckle, make a note of what hole it is on, unfasten and wipe over it, and then immediately rebuckle it.
6. Wipe over the bit with the wet sponge.
7. If it is soiled with dried-on dirt, you may have to soak the bit in warm water to loosen it.
8. Apply saddle soap, unfastening and refastening the buckles and billets as you go. Try not to get too much soap near any stitching because these are best left as dry as possible.

Note: Never use household soap as saddle soap—it is a VERY different product. Saddle soap not only cleans the leather, but it also contains glycerine and waxes to feed, protect, and waterproof it. It comes in different forms: spray, creamy liquid, soap bars, and in tubs.

Synthetic saddles do not need soaping; simply brush off the hairs and wipe them with a damp, soapy sponge.

▲ **Your tack is the link** *between you and your horse. You don't want brittle or greasy leather chafing his skin.*

TIP If you do a lot of competing, it may be helpful to have a rough bridle and a show bridle that is only kept for special events.

1

2

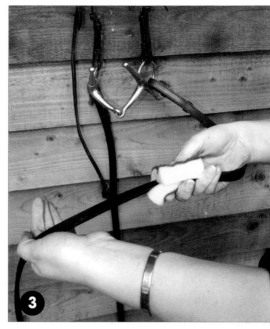

3

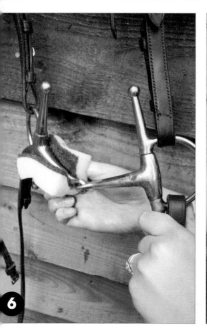

6

7

8

Turning out

It pays to stay safe when leading your horse out. A horse that barges into you or drags you will soon learn that he can get away. Good manners are essential.

1. When entering the stable, push your horse's chest and say "back" to move him away from the door.
2. Slip on the halter or headcollar, but make sure he stays back and does not crush you against the door in his eagerness to get out.
3. Open the door wide, and go out just ahead of him.
4. Stay just in front of his shoulder when leading him. It is traditional to walk on the left of the horse.
5. When entering the field, walk through the gate and then turn your horse to face it as you close it (*below*).
6. Remove the headcollar with the horse still facing the closed gate before saying "off you go" or something similar so he knows that he is free to go.

Never release a horse that is facing into the field – he may bolt off to see his friends with you still holding the rope.

CATCHING YOUR HORSE

Some horses are little devils about being caught! If you are rushing to get your horse in to saddle up for a ride, or because bad weather suddenly sweeps in, it can be infuriating having to walk endless laps around the paddock in an attempt to catch him. You need to have some tricks up your sleeve to gain the upper hand.

DO

* Spend time in the field with your horse and use it to bond with him by giving him a treat, or a rub, or some personal attention while you are picking up droppings.
* Catch your horse as a prelude to doing pleasant things. Take him out of the field for a feed (a couple of carrots perhaps) and then return him to the field without working him.
* If you know he is hard to catch, fence off the field into several small paddocks so that he can't get too far away from you.
* Keep your body language friendly –

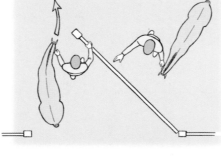

◀ **Do not let your horse barge** *out of the stable. Say "back" and move him away from the door.*

approach your horse from the side heading toward his shoulder, rather than head-on, and keep your eyes and arms lowered.

- Reward your horse with a treat once you have the headcollar on him.
- Be persistent. If your horse realizes that you will give up quickly, he is more likely to be difficult. If he knows you will keep going until you do catch him, he may feel that he would rather not exhaust himself.

DON'T

- Don't allow anyone to aggravate or tease horses in the field or they will steer clear of anyone who is approaching them.
- Don't enter a field with a feed bowl unless there is only one horse in it, otherwise you'll be mobbed and may be trampled. Keep any treats hidden in your pocket.
- Don't just catch your horse in order to ride him. He

may start to dread you coming if he is always taken away from the field to work.

- Don't leave a headcollar on your horse in the field unless it is made of leather (which will break under pressure) or it is a specially-designed safety headcollar. An unbreakable halter could get caught on an object and lead to the horse injuring himself quite badly.
- Don't flap the headcollar or march up to a horse aggressively.
- Don't smack or shout at a horse once you catch him – even if it has taken you an hour and you are furious.

▲ **You will rarely tire** *a horse by chasing after him to catch him – you will be the one who ends up worn out!*

◀◀ **Approach from the side** *and walk toward the shoulder with eyes and arms lowered.*

◀ **Fencing off the field** *into several smaller paddocks will stop your horse from running too far away.*

FEEDING AND NUTRITION

All horses should be treated as individuals when it comes to feeding because their age, build, and breeding or "type," as well as the workload they are being asked to do, have a huge bearing on their dietary needs.

- Some horses can almost live on fresh air – these are termed easy keepers.
- Others can be fed large volumes of highly nutritious feeds but still look like a bag of bones – these are known as poor keepers.

Although it is not a hard and fast rule, easy keepers tend to have more laid-back characters, whereas poor keepers can often be worriers or have sharper, more edgy personalities.

Assessing condition: If you run your hand over the side of a horse or pony it should feel smooth, but you should still be able to feel some of his ribs just below the surface of the skin. A thin horse will have prominent ribs, a bony rump, and a "tucked up" appearance. An overweight horse may have pads of fat along the crest of his neck and over his shoulder (just in front of where the knee rolls are on the saddle). He is also likely to have a huge backside!

You may think that your horse lacks energy and increase the quantity of feed you give him in the hope that it will pep up activity levels. However, this is not the case because both an underweight and an overweight horse may appear lethargic. Balanced nutrition is needed to add condition slowly and to bring an underweight horse back into shape. Simply increasing rations will not speed up an overweight horse – he needs to shed weight and build muscle tone through increased exercise to become more forward-going.

Remember: A weigh tape is a useful tool to keep an eye on changes in weight, so why not see just how heavy your horse really is! Use it to measure your horse's girth and then read off the probable weight from the scale printed on the tape.

◀ **Visit your horse daily,** *and supplement his grass with feed if necessary.*

Very poor condition

Poor condition

Moderate condition

TIP

Horses prefer several smaller meals to one huge one. Also, by providing carrots and roughage, you will keep him chewing longer.

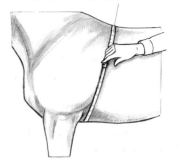

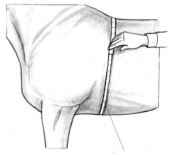

▼ **A weigh tape is useful** to calculate your horse's approximate weight.

Position it across the base of the withers and around, close to the elbow.

Too far back (like this) will give a false reading.

▲ **A quick glance isn't enough.** *Learn to see and feel weight change that may occur gradually. Feel for the ribs and for pads of fat.*

▲ **Nutrition is an art** *that requires careful balancing according to your horse's condition and workload. You will probably have to make changes throughout the year.*

Good condition

Fat condition

Very fat condition

Components of the diet

Fiber: Keeps the "engine" of the gut functioning properly. It is found in all forage – grass, hay, haylage, and chaffs.

Protein: The building blocks of the body's cells, protein is needed for a horse to grow, to build muscle, and to repair damaged tissues after strain or injury. It is found in many grains and fresh grass.

Carbohydrates: These are organic compounds that occur in food, such as sugars, starch, and cellulose. Roughly 75 percent of all plant material is a type of carbohydrate, and it is the primary source of energy for a horse. It is found in grains and fresh grass.

Fats: Fats provide a lot of calories for energy. If they are not used up through physical activity, they can be laid down as fat in the body and cause weight gain. They are found in oils present in cereals or can be added to the diet in liquid form (*below*).

Vitamins and minerals: These are organic compounds that are vital for the overall good condition of the body. They also are present in green plants and cereals. They help to keep horses healthy.

Forage: Forage should be the mainstay of the diet. This may be grass, hay, or short or long chop (e.g., alfalfa or straw chaff).

Remember: If you are changing the type of food that you feed your horse, make the change gradually. It takes time for the bacteria in your horse's gut that aid the process of digestion to adjust to breaking down different foods. Begin by replacing part of the old food with a handful of new food, and then build up to the new diet over a period of three or four days.

▼ **Forage should always be the mainstay of the diet.** *From grass to dried alfalfa, forage comes in many forms.*

◀ **Horses will naturally** *nibble at herbs, bushes, and trees if they are given the opportunity.*

▼ **Because hay will make up** *the bulk of your horse's ration, inspect it carefully before purchase.*

Straw-based chaff

Mixed food

Pellets

Alfalfa chaff

▲ **A selection of chaffs** *plus carrots can make an interesting high-fiber feed without grains.*

◀ **There are endless varieties of** *grasses, mixes, and pelleted feeds available. Every bag of feed will list the content analysis and should suggest the type of animal to which it is best suited.*

Preparing and giving feed

A horse should eat between 2 percent and 4 percent of his overall bodyweight each day, depending on breed, type, and workload. Therefore, an average 1100 lb (500 kg) horse may require approximately 27.5 lb (12.5 kg) of food per day.

Weight Guidelines
SMALL BALE OF HAY between 55-77 lb (25-35 kg)
ROUND SCOOP OF CHAFF Approx 10 oz (300 g)
ROUND SCOOP OF OATS/CUBES Approx 4.4 lb (2 kg)

When calculating how much to feed:

- Be aware that the percentage figure includes all the grass/hay that your horse will consume in addition to any concentrates.
- Remember that a scoop of chaff weighs much less than a similar scoop of mix, so weigh out the feed until you are familiar with the amounts – guesswork won't do!

Use a weigh tape to assess your horse's overall bodyweight, and remeasure him every month to monitor weight fluctuations. Observe him while he eats for signs of quidding (dropping excessive amounts of food from the mouth, usually a sign of a dental problem). Take notice of his droppings. If they are excessively runny or have whole grains or long fibers present in them, this may be a sign of poor digestion. Maintain a good deworming routine or your horse will not enjoy the full benefit of the expensive food you are giving him and could suffer permanent gut damage.

HAY

Do choose good-quality hay. It should smell fresh and not be too brittle or dusty. Know the source of your hay so that you can be confident that it does not contain dangerous weeds.

Do not use hay that is overly dusty, smells stale, or has areas of mold, which could lead to breathing problems.

Do store hay in a dry, airy space. Keep it covered to prevent contamination from birds, rodents or cats.

Do feed hay loose on the floor or in a hay net or low-mounted trough. A high-set hay rack is not ideal because this feeding position is unnatural – horses naturally eat with their heads lowered. Also, dust can more easily be breathed in or get in the horse's eyes causing various health problems. Advice on how to tie up a hay net can be found on pages 60 to 61.

Do soak hay if it is at all dusty, but only for five to ten minutes. Longer soaking would remove some of the precious nutrients.

▶ *A typical diet may comprise hay and commercial feeds.*
1. Measure or weigh out the feed into the bowl.
2. Add any supplements, herbs, or tonics if required.
3. Just before feeding, dampen with water to help digestion (do not add water too early unless you want to soften the feed because cubes will begin to disintegrate).
4. Finally, stir the mix well.

TIP Keep feeding simple. Manufacturers do the hard work by designing specific diets for different horses so you don't have to worry!

▲ **If hay needs soaking** to make it less dusty, submerge it for around five minutes. You may need to put a weight on it to stop it from floating up.

▶ **Hay should be fed** off the ground or at a low level to limit dust inhalation.

Roughage and concentrates

Roughage (hay, grass, and other high-fiber feed sources) is the healthiest and most natural feed for horses. It's also a great way to keep your horse busy and constantly chewing—eating it takes up more time than eating concentrated grains. Concentrates (hard feed) are foodstuffs that are low in fiber but high in other nutrients. Grains and grain by-products, pelleted food, and cereals are typical examples. Listed below are some guidelines on how best to use them.

Do use a wall-mounted feed manger or a flexible container that will not cause injury if left in the stable.

Do not use a standard bucket (*right*) because the horse could get his headcollar caught up in the handle or be injured if the plastic splits.

Do store feed in rodent-proof storage bins. Sweep up any spillage so as not to attract vermin.

Do check the "use by" dates on the sacks of feed and use them in rotation. Discard any feed that is out of date or that has gotten damp.

Do divide the day's ration into several small meals. Horses are grazers and are designed to feed little and often to gain the most benefit from their food.

Do make changes to the diet gradually over a period of three to four days by replacing a proportion of the old ration with the new feed and gradually building it up to the full volume of the new feed ration.

Do have a noticeboard visible where you can post your horse's feeding routine for others to follow in your absence.

Remember: If you are feeding a lot of chaff, it is beneficial to moisten the feed slightly with a little water to make it less dusty and easier for the horse to swallow. A watering can gives you greater control than splashing water in from a bucket.

YUM!

Succulents like carrots and apples are a real favorite, especially when grazing is limited. Carrots are full of fiber and can be fed in high volume without producing a hyperactive horse – a bucket full of carrots will keep a horse satisfied without making him fat. Keep them whole so that he has to spend time chewing them up or, if you must cut them, only slice them lengthways, never in rings because they can get stuck in his throat.

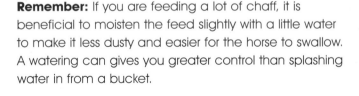

KEEP FEEDING SIMPLE

Commercially-prepared feed should not need to be supplemented with vitamins if it is fed at the recommended levels (guidelines are usually on the bags). You do not need shelves full of supplements, herbs, and tonics – they only complicate matters!

A mineral or salt lick should be available at all times in the pasture or stable.

FEEDING IN A FIELD

When feeding horses at pasture, tie them up individually to the fence if they are likely to squabble. Place feed bowls at least two horse lengths apart, and watch them at all times. Horses are notoriously greedy and aggressive when feeding, so stay at a safe distance and carry a training whip if necessary to make them back off if you need to.

▼ **After pouring the feed** *into bins, label the lid of each bin with its contents to avoid guesswork.*

▲ **A rubber feed tub** *is safest because it won't split if the horse tramples it.*

◄ **Competing may** *mean a long day out, so take your horse's feed with you.*

◄◄ **When feeding in a field,** *spread feeds widely apart so horses will not squabble or miss out.*

Feeding guidelines

PLEASURE HORSE (LIGHT WORK)

This is a horse or pony ridden about three times a week and rarely pushed to exert himself for any long periods. Most of his "fuel" should come from grazing or forage with any vitamin or mineral shortfalls being supplemented.

Daily ration: 2 to 2.5 percent of bodyweight

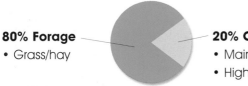

80% Forage
• Grass/hay

20% Concentrates
• Maintenance mix
• High-fibre cubes

Dietary Extras • Succulents
• Fresh (or dried) herbs

• Turn out as much as possible
• Hawthorn, rosebay willowherb, and rose hips

4-H HORSE/SHOW JUMPING HORSE/SHOW HORSE

An active horse but one who may only be required to work hard on weekends, with several days off work each week, may predispose him to weight gain. A higher energy mix could be used on the days where he is working hard, reverting back to high-fiber cubes on rest days.

Daily ration: 2 to 2.5 percent of bodyweight

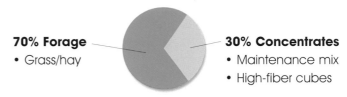

70% Forage
• Grass/hay

30% Concentrates
• Maintenance mix
• High-fiber cubes

Dietary Extras • Succulents
• Fresh (or dried) herbs

• Turn out as much as possible, in paddock if necessary
• Hawthorn, garlic, cleavers, and meadowsweet are useful herbs

POOR KEEPER OR HYPER TYPE

Often of Thoroughbred ancestry, these types may cause a problem because forage alone does not provide the calorie intake they require to maintain a good weight. Yet too much energy will make their already exuberant character unmanageable. Turning them out for as long as possible will help them to relax and allow them to expend some energy. The slightest distraction or a stressful situation will hamper their nutrient absorption still further. Yeast or probiotics added to the diet will assist in optimum gut function.

TIP Leave a mineral lick out for a "good keeper" on a forage diet to ensure he gets the full spectrum of vitamins, but check it does not get devoured in just one day!

Daily ration: 2.5 to 3 percent of bodyweight

70% Forage
• Grass/hay

30% Concentrates
• Conditioning mix
• Alfalfa/lucerne
• Probiotics • Oil

Dietary Extras • Succulents
• Fresh (or dried) herbs

• Turn out as much as possible
• Valerian, hawthorn, chamomile, and meadowsweet are useful herbs

EVENT HORSE (HARD WORK)

These horses work consistently hard across a wide spectrum of activities that require precision as well as power. They may find it hard to switch off and recharge their batteries, so it is essential to assist their mental and physical well-being to achieve optimum results.

Daily ration: 2.5 percent of bodyweight

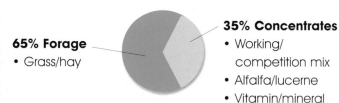

65% Forage
• Grass/hay

35% Concentrates
• Working/ competition mix
• Alfalfa/lucerne
• Vitamin/mineral supplement
• Probiotics • Oil

Dietary Extras • Succulents
• Fresh (or dried) herbs

• Turn out as much as possible
• Electrolytes may be needed occasionally
• Ginkgo biloba, watercress, dandelions, beech, and hazel branches enhance the diet
• Whole corn cobs (maize) provide energy as well as stimulation while being eaten

VETERAN OVER 20 YEARS (RETIRED OR SEMI-RETIRED)

Older animals often have a decreased ability to absorb nutrients effectively. They may lose condition and have problems chewing due to worn or loose teeth. Despite their light workload, they need higher sources of energy/calories and also good available protein and calcium. If they have trouble eating hay or grass, high-fiber cubes can be fed with sugar beet pulp to provide fiber.

Daily ration: 2 to 2.5 percent of bodyweight

70% Forage
• Grass/hay

30% Concentrates
• Veteran/conditioning mix
• High-fiber cubes
• Alfalfa
• Oil
• Sugar beet pulp
• Probiotics/yeast

Dietary Extras • Succulents
• Fresh (or dried) herbs

• High calcium, high protein
• Turn out as much as possible
• Cider vinegar is a useful addition to the diet
• Willow, meadowsweet, and comfrey are useful herbs for animals with arthritis

Hay nets

Even if you feed hay from the floor or a manger, there are times when you will need to use a hay net, perhaps when your horse has to wait outside for the farrier for a long time or to keep him occupied when traveling in a trailer. Tying a hay net safely is a very important thing to learn.

1. Fill the hay net and gather up the cord to close it.
2. Thread the end of the cord through the tie ring in the stable/trailer and pull the hay net up until the center of it is level with the horse's chest.
3. Thread the cord through the net as low down as possible; this will help to stabilize the net as it gets emptied by the horse eating the contents.
4. Bring the cord back up toward the tie ring, and tie it in a quick-release knot (as shown below). The weight of the net will keep it taut, but you will still be able to release it quickly and easily if you need to.
5. Finally, turn the whole hay net around so that the knot is at the back of the net.

Too high – the horse is straining unnaturally to reach the hay, and seeds and dust could fall in his eyes.
Too low – the net flaps around and the pony could get caught up in it.

Ultra-Quick-Release Knot

1. Thread the cords through the tie ring, then the net, and pull up to the required height.
2. Make a loop and hold it with your left hand.
3. With your right hand, pass the free end behind the hanging cord, and then forward through the loop, making a second loop.
4. Release the first loop with your second hand, and pull down on the second loop. This will make the knot tight. The free end can be threaded through this loop for extra security.

SOAKING HAY

If you need to soak your hay, a hay net will make life much easier. Use a large container filled with water and submerge the hay net for 10 minutes to minimize the danger of dust and spores being carried out of the hay by draughts of wind. Hang the hay net up on a fence to drain; this will make it much lighter to carry and stop the stable bedding from getting wet or your legs from getting soaked as you carry it to the place where you are going to secure it.

▲ **A hay net may look** *full, but it is the weight of food that you supply, not the volume, that is important.*

▲ **Tie the net high** *but below the horse's eye level. Use a quick-release knot so it is easy to refill.*

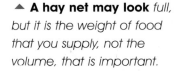

◀ **Soak hay only** on the day it is being used because damp hay can soon turn moldy. Submerge for five to ten minutes (no longer or the nutrients will seep out). Hang up to drain **outside** the stable for a few minutes or you will soak the bedding. Change the soaking water every couple of days.

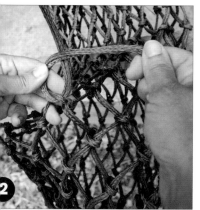

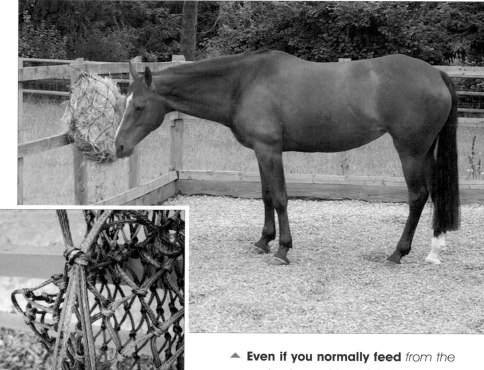

▲ **Even if you normally feed** from the ground, a hay net is useful when you are traveling or when your horse is tied up waiting for some period of time.

PROBLEMS? WE HAVE THE ANSWERS

I DON'T HAVE TIME TO RIDE

This is a common problem, and it can be frustrating and weigh on your conscience knowing you are not giving your horse enough exercise. It only takes a few weeks for a horse to become unfit and put on weight if he is out at grass. If he is stabled, confinement for long periods of time can lead to stress and depression, which reveals itself in the form of stable vices (such as cribbing, windsucking, and boxwalking) and sometimes aggressive behavior.

Even if you have limited time, you can give your horse some valuable physical exercise by longeing or loose schooling him (see below for explanations of these terms). You will save time because:

• The horse or pony does not need to be wearing any tack (other than a halter for loose schooling or a longeing cavesson headcollar), therefore you save time getting ready.

• Because you are not riding and full riding attire is not required (except for a helmut in case you are knocked over and gloves for holding the longeing rope), you

should not get sweaty or dirty, so you can go straight out afterward without needing to wash or change.

Just spending as little as ten minutes a day either longeing or loose schooling your horse will almost certainly reap great benefits.

Loose schooling requires a round pen, corral, or arena. You don't even need to spend time fitting a longe line. It is quite possible to sit in the middle of the corral simply shouting "trot on" and flicking a whip occasionally. The horse gets exercised, and you can read or do some homework while he is working.

IF YOU DON'T HAVE TIME TO RIDE, SHARE YOUR HORSE

For the average owner, it is often very hard to find enough hours in the day to keep a horse or pony well exercised, mentally stimulated, and properly fed and cared for, in addition to all the chores owning a horse entails. A good solution is to share your horse with another rider. He or she can lavish care and attention on him when you are not around, and your horse will benefit from the extra exercise and fuss that he will receive from an additional person. They may even help out with the boring chores, too!

It is important to choose this person carefully and be certain that they are responsible and sufficiently capable, or that they will have any necessary assistance or be supervised by a responsible adult. You may find your horse improves in both temperament and performance if, say, he has the benefit of exercising with two riders – for instance, one who is prepared to put in the time schooling and improving his jumping ability, and another who simply enjoys a quiet ride.

▲ **Stable vices are often caused** by lack of mental or physical stimulation.

▲ **Poor management** of this horse has caused him to be depressed.

◀ **Longeing is a** type of exercise in which a horse is attached to a long rope and moves around the handler in a circular path.

▼ **There is no line** in loose schooling, but often a round pen is used to keep the horse contained while he exercises.

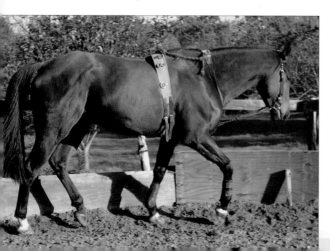

I don't have time to ride

Longeing can be done in any type of arena or in an open field. The horse wears a longeing cavesson (a padded headcollar with three swiveling rings on the front of the noseband). A long rope called a longe line (usually about 35 ft /10.5 m long) is clipped to a ring on the noseband to link the horse to the handler.

1. The only equipment you need is a helmut and, most essentially, gloves. Without gloves you can get nasty rope burns if the horse pulls against you and causes the rope to run swiftly though your hands.
2. Adjust the longeing cavesson so it fits snugly around the horse's head. If it is loose, it will rub as the horse moves and may even slip over his eyes, which would make the horse very sore.
3. Attach the longe line to the center ring on the noseband. (You could use the side ring nearest to you, but then you must remember to change it to the other side if you change the direction in which the horse is traveling).
4. Take the loose end of the longe line in your left hand, bend your arm up, and collect the slack in the rope with your right hand, wrapping it over your left arm – from hand to elbow, hand to elbow – until it is at a manageable length.
5. Face your horse sideways in the direction you want him to go. As you face him, you should hold the slack of the rope in the hand nearest his head and the longe whip in the hand nearest his tail.
6. Keep the whip low and move it slowly to encourage him to move off. There is no need to "crack" it sharply or your horse may jump out of the arena in surprise!
7. Release the slack until the horse is moving out on a circle large enough for the pace he is doing (about 20 ft/6 m for trotting and 30 ft/9 m for cantering).
8. Use voice commands delivered in a high pitch to

quicken the pace – "TROT ON"– and in a low pitch to slow him down – "W-H-O-A."
9. Ensure you exercise him evenly on both reins, working around the circle in both directions.

(A) *Keep your body facing your horse's belly and the whip pointed at his tail when requesting forward movement, and maintain this arc.*

(B) *To slow him, angle yourself in front of the movement, facing his head. Pointing the whip at his shoulder will prevent him from turning in.*

▼ **Moving your position** *further behind your horse will encourage him forward if he is lazy.*

A

B

◀ **Check that the cavesson** fits snugly so it will not move during exercise and rub. The line is attached to one of the rings on the front of the horse's nose. Coil the excess rope up so it does not tangle.

▼ **Use voice commands.** Horses learn very quickly, and it is rewarding to get a reaction without using the whip.

My horse has scared me – I don't want to

The pattern of horse ownership rarely runs smoothly. Horses and riders both have "off days," but you must not let a bad experience discourage you.

Everybody falls off! Your horse may shy at a bird in a bush, put in a nasty buck before a canter, or dump you in front of a show jump. It really DOES happen to everyone, so don't be despondent.

1. Establish some ground rules
- Take charge of your horse on the ground. You need to be the boss (firm but fair, of course) in your relationship.

Goal: Practice some groundwork skills.
- Backing the horse up establishes that he cannot encroach on your personal space.
- Moving his quarters by fingertip pressure on his sides will make him more responsive.

- Practice trotting him alongside you, halting, and then making him back up – you want quick reactions from him.

2. Believe you both can succeed
If you are having problems jumping or lack confidence in your ability as a rider, it helps to assess both your ability and your horse's abilities separately.

Goal: Gain confidence from good experiences.
- Have a few lessons on several other horses; then you **know** you can cope in different situations or jump successfully when you need to.
- Get an experienced rider to ride and train your horse to address his problems. Watch how he behaves, and how the rider deals with any hiccups.
- Now that you and your horse have both gained in confidence, skill, and experience, you are ready to put the partnership together under the guidance of an instructor.

◀ **Don't let one bad** *experience make you fearful of progressing with your riding skills.*

ide him!

◀ **Riding should be fun,** *not stressful. Ask for help if you are nervous or confused.*

▶ **It may help to watch someone else** *ride your horse and prove to you that he is up to the task.*

◤ **Backing up a horse** *puts* **you** *in the "alpha" dominant position.*

▼ **Making him yield** *to pressure will help on the ground and in the saddle.*

He won't let me catch him in the field

Never underestimate the intelligence of horses! They will see you a mile away, and if they don't want to be brought in from the field they certainly will give you the run around! Here are some useful do's and don't's to help you overcome this problem if you have a horse that loves to give you a hard time.

Don't always just catch your horse to ride him or he may start to resent you because you are interrupting his freedom to make him "work."

Do catch him to give him a stroke or a treat, or just to say hello.

Don't enter a field full of horses with a feed bowl or you will be mobbed.

Do carry a treat hidden in a pocket that only your horse will get. He'll learn to look forward to your special attention.

Don't march up to your horse waving your halter – you'll seem threatening to him and he may run off.

Do keep your arms low (hiding the halter if necessary) and eyes looking down so you appear submissive.

Don't approach him directly from the front or creep up behind him to surprise him.

Do approach at an angle level with his shoulder so he can see you clearly.

Don't immediately attempt to get the halter over his nose as soon as you reach him.

Do stand at his shoulder, feed the treat with one hand, and then slip the rope over his neck with the other.

Don't hurry or your sense of panic may transmit itself to the horse, and you may annoy him by being rough.

Do gently pass the halter over his nose and head calmly and quietly.

Do stroke him on the neck and talk nicely to him as you lead him away.

TIP: To overcome the problem of horses that are terrible to catch, it is important to spend lots of time with them in the field, approaching them regularly, and then walking away again so they do not believe they will be caught each time that you approach. A leather or safety halter can be left on them when they are in the field to give you a further advantage in that you will have something secure to grab onto.

TIP Spend time in the field just "horse watching." You will learn how horses interact, and they will see you as part of the herd.

◄◄ **Marching head-on** *toward your horse swinging the halter can seem threatening to him.*

◄ **A nervous horse** *is quickly on his toes and much faster than you!*

◢ **Approach your horse** *from the side so he can see you, and walk slowly with eyes and arms down.*

▼ **Slip the rope** *over his neck, and then put on the halter without being rough or in a rush.*

I need to improve my handling skills

Horses are herd animals and, in their natural environment, would soon find their rank in the herd, some being more dominant and some more docile and subservient. As handlers and riders, we become part of their herd, and so we need to establish our status as their caregiver and leader in a sympathetic manner that earns their respect but does not provoke fear.

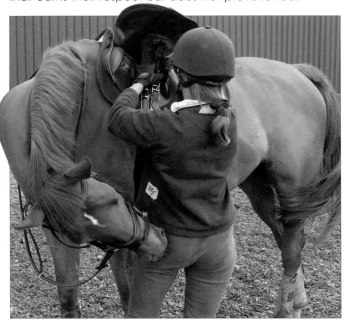

Problems that can arise from poor handling can include: being dragged, the horse running off when being led, barging out of the stable, acting aggressively when being fed, biting, kicking, and general boisterous behavior. Try to follow these guidelines to avoid problems like these cropping up in your relationship with your horse.

- Always move around horses in a purposeful manner. Horses can easily pick up on any nervousness that is felt by their handlers, and this can create skittish behavior like pulling back when being tied up or fidgeting as you put on a blanket, whereas a confident, systematic approach will exude calmness and provide reassurance to the horse.

- Always approach horses in a way that gives them plenty of visual or audible warning that you are coming. If you approach them from behind, say their name, or speak some form of greeting so that you do not startle them.

- When dealing with a dominant animal, wear gloves, a helmut, and sturdy boots at all times. Carry a whip to create distance between you should he try to barge out or run into you.

- Practice backing up a dominant horse. A dominant horse will chase off or threaten other horses to get them to back away from food, etc., and this establishes respect. Gain similar respect by doing likewise. You may have to begin by pushing his chest or tapping a whip on the ground, but eventually just saying "back" or marching toward your horse with a dominant posture should be enough to get him to move away.

- When you enter the stable, make your horse back away from the door. This will limit his ability either to barge out past you or crush you against the door as you bolt it behind you.

- When you feed your horse in the stable, do not allow him to snatch at the feed as you bring it in. Make him back away, and place the bucket down or fill the manger before you allow him to approach it.

- Allow your horse time to see, approach, and sniff any new object (like blankets, brushes, feed buckets) that might alarm him if they are suddenly used near him.

TIP Attaching the lead rope to the side ring on the halter will give you more leverage when you are leading a powerful, strong horse.

- Talk calmly around horses. Stroke and scratch them on the neck, shoulder, and withers rather than patting them, which is actually nothing less than a little slap.
- Do not regularly feed tidbits from your pockets or your horse will expect them and begin to hound you for them (potentially chewing your pockets to get at them). He may well get grumpy if you have forgotten them one day!

Remember: Ask for help if you are having difficulties. A nervous horse being looked after by a nervous, inexperienced handler is not a good combination. Understanding horse language comes with experience, so never pass up the offer of guidance from an experienced person. It may prevent an accident in the future.

TIP: When leading a strong horse, keep his head close and slightly turned toward you. Do not let him get in front of you. Having his head facing slightly toward you means that his quarters will be angled slightly away from you; this will limit any chance of him kicking out at you.

◀ **Bracing your elbow** *into your horse's neck gives you more leverage when leading.*

▼ **Barging is bad manners.** *Insist your horse goes back when you enter the stable with his feed.*

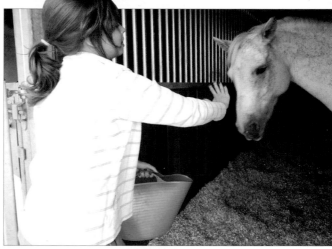

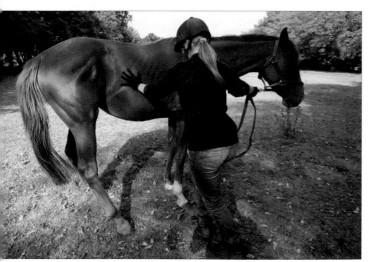

◀◀ **Clumsy or boisterous** *horses need to learn that only **you** can push **them** around. Mimic the action of a dominant horse.*

◀ **Backing up** *a horse keeps him out of your space and asserts your authority.*

KEEPING YOUR HORSE FIT

FIT FOR THE SHOW RING

Having a good show horse is not simply a case of arriving at an event with a horse in good conformation who is well-groomed – although presentation does play a big part. A show horse should have good core strength to be able to carry himself well and feel light to ride and easy to control. A show horse is likely to carry slightly more weight than one used for other more athletic disciplines and have a good top line of muscle tone.

Obedience and suppleness are needed rather than just stamina, so training will play a big part in getting your horse in shape for the show ring.

- A SHOW HORSE needs exercise for three to five days a week. It should consist of slow controled work, plus relaxed hacking (*above*) so this level of exercise is easily achievable by most riders.
- RIDE LOTS OF TRANSITIONS, which will get your horse to be more responsive and light in the rein contact.
- CIRCLES AND SERPENTINES will improve suppleness and help if you have to do an individual show at a competition.

- WORKING LONG AND LOW will release tension in your horse's back and help to create a strong top line rather than a forced outline.
- ALWAYS WARM UP AND COOL DOWN gradually to avoid the risk of muscle strains.
- KEEP YOUR HORSE ENTERTAINED to prevent him from becoming stale by varying your training routine regularly to keep him sharp.
- FREQUENT GROOMING will dispel dust and make your horse gleam as well as creating those "feel good" benefits of massaging his muscles.

Feeding: A diet made up of 80 to 95 percent forage, plus a mix concentrate feed is ideal. Adding corn oil will add weight (if needed) and bring a gleam to his coat.

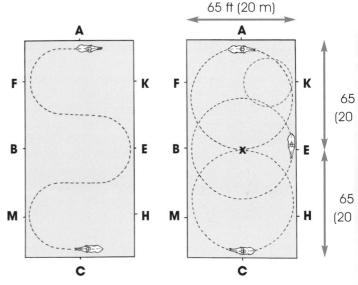

▲ **A serpentine** *links semi-circles and changes of direction to keep your horse supple and responsive to your aids.*

▲ **Circles can be done** *at many points in the arena. Pay attention to making an accurate shape whatever the size.*

TIP To avoid spooky behavior at an event, get your horse accustomed to the sights and sounds of a show ring by staging a mock show with your friends.

◀ **Fitting a roller** *and elastic side reins will help build muscle.*

▶ **Working long and low** *makes the horse stretch and use his top line.*

▼ **The side reins** *help the horse step into the contact rather than falling on the forehand.*

Fit for show jumping

A horse predominantly used for show jumping needs to be powerful enough to cope with the exertions asked of him and light enough not to put undue pressure on his joints, ligaments, and tendons from the impact of landing after a jump. A show jumper has to put in short bursts of athletic energy – this is very different from the low-impact exercise expected of a show horse or the sustained periods of stamina required by an eventer or endurance horse.

- A SHOW JUMPER needs to be exercised five or six times a week, although it is crucial to examine legs daily for signs of strains/injury that could be worsened by exercise.
- CORE STRENGTH can be achieved through training. Practice collection and extension in each pace to improve lightness and responsiveness.
- RAISED POLES AND HILL WORK will increase muscle tone in the hind legs for improved strength of propulsion and power on take off.
- SHORT BURSTS OF CANTER and gallop on a hack will keep him fresh and help him stretch his frame fully.
- JUMPING a variety of uprights and spread fences at home will give you both confidence and help you succeed when in competition.

Feeding: A diet made up of 70 to 80 percent forage, plus a working or competition mix is ideal. Alfalfa and sugar beet would be a good base for the mix. Remember to cut down on the amount of concentrates that you supply on days off.

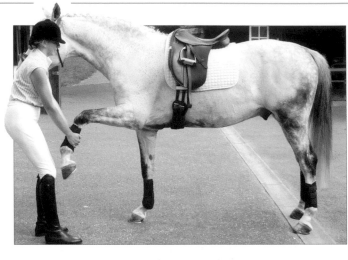

▲ **Loosen up your horse** *with massage and stretching exercises before work.*

▼ **Vary the workload.** *A horse can become stale if his life is purely show jumping.*

TIP Make short-term goals, as well as long-term goals, and draw up a timetable of when you will ride and the exercises planned for each week.

▲ **Longeing over poles** boosts the horse's confidence because he can solve striding patterns while unencumbered by a rider.

◀◀ ◀ **Raised poles** and asymmetric grids will keep your horse alert and prevent him from rushing.

SHOW PRESENTATION

It is always encouraging to be told that your horse looks fabulous, so let us look at some tricks and skills needed for stylish show presentation to transform a scruffy horse into a competition winner.

1. Bathe your horse

- In addition to general dust and grime, horses that are shedding or changing coats will often look scruffy. By giving them a thorough bath, initially with an antibacterial shampoo and thereafter with a mild equine shampoo, you will enhance the appearance of the coat. Don't forget his mane and tail too! *(See the section on how to bathe a horse on pages 36-37.)*

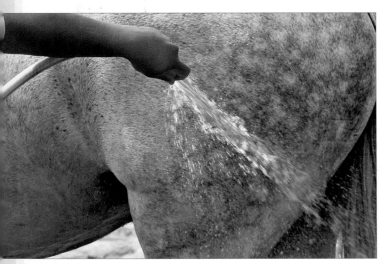

2. Trim up your horse

- A straggly looking tail, unkempt mane, and a hairy head will do nothing to give the impression of a quality horse.
- Trim the whiskers and any hairs under the jaw.
- Trim any hairs that protrude from the ears.
- Cutting the hairs away from the heels gives a sharper outline.

Tail: Ask someone to place their arm under the dock of your horse's tail. This will give the approximate height at which it will be carried when he is moving actively. Now cut the bottom of the tail so that it finishes 3 to 4 in (8 to 10 cm) below the level of his hock.

3. Plait your horse

- Trim or pull the mane to a length of about 4 to 5 in (10 to 13 cm) long and wash both the mane and tail a couple of days before the show. Newly washed hair is too slippery to plait!
  (For instructions on how to plait a mane or tail see pages 78-81).

4. Finishing touches

- Add hoof oil to clean dry hooves and to make them shine.
- A little baby oil or highlighter cream on the muzzle and around the eyes will enhance the face.
- Baby oil or detangler spray brushed through the tail will keep it silky and knot-free.
- How about some quarter marks? A chessboard effect or a star or two on his quarters and he will stand out from the crowd.

◀ **Bathing gets rid** *of sweat and dust that makes the coat dull.*

▶ **By brushing** *against the lie of the hair, a stencil can be used to give a stunning effect on the hindquarters.*

◀ **Cut the tail squarely** *across for a neat appearance. Normally 3 to 4 in (8 to 10 cm) below the hock is about the right length, but don't be too scissor-happy!*

◀ **Trimming parts** *like the heels, coronet, ears, and whiskers give a sharper outline, which helps to give your horse a classier appearance.*

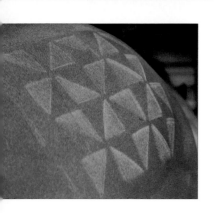

▲ **This horse just exudes** *quality and good health with his gleaming coat and perfect presentation.*

▶ **Bandages look sharp** *but may have to be removed before going into the show ring.*

How to plait a mane

Does your horse look like he has been dragged through a hedge backwards? Do your plaits look like a row of angry hedgehogs having a fight, rather than elegant braids? Here's how to improve the situation and produce a beautiful plaited mane.

What you will need:
- Elastic plaiting bands (the same color as the mane)
- Comb
- Hair gel

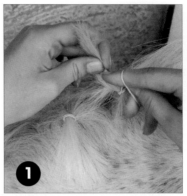

1. Aim to have an odd number of plaits (11 or 13 is usual) along the offside (right) side of the neck, plus one on the forelock. Divide the mane into equal sections about as wide as the palm of your hand. Put a band loosely around each to keep them separate before you begin to plait.

2. It is normally easier to start near the ears because it is easier to adjust the lower sections if you have to make any adjustments toward the end of the whole job of plaiting the mane. Take the first section, comb it through, and if there are any spiky hairs along the crest, smooth them down with gel. Divide the section into three equal portions.

3. Begin plaiting by crossing the right and left sections alternately over the middle section. Keep the plait as tight as possible for a tidy effect.

4. Plait as far down as you possibly can, until you only have a few thin hairs remaining.

5. Put a band tightly around the base of the plait, and fold the loose ends in before looping the band around again to give a neat end.

6. Fold the plait in half underneath itself so the end faces back to the crest. Secure with a band.

7. Roll or fold the plait back underneath to make a tight ball tucked into the crest of the mane. Smooth down any stray hairs, and wrap a final elastic band around it to secure the ball.

   Work your way down the sections, trying to keep each "ball" the same size and at the same level as the others. As you reach the withers, you may have to use a wider section of hair to get the same size "ball," but be careful that you do not plait too tightly against the neck or it may pull painfully as the horse moves.

TIP It's neater to have too many plaits that look small than too few plaits as large as tennis balls!

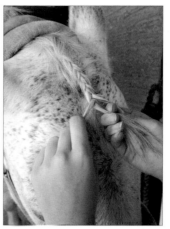

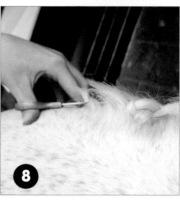

▲ ◥ Comb the forelock forward and start with a French braid taking sections of hair from each side. Then plait right to the end of the forelock. Roll the plait once for a longer braid or twice for a ball, and secure with a band.

▼ A horse's neck can be greatly enhanced by clever plaiting of his mane. Set the plaits high if your horse has an underdeveloped neck or low if he has a thick crest. It really works beautifully as a finishing touch.

8. If there are a few stray hairs remaining, you may want to trim these off completely to give a sleek line from withers to the first plait.

Finish by plaiting the forelock and rolling it up into a neat ball too. Wow! How sharp does he look now?

Caution: Although using a needle and thread to secure the plait in a ball is tidier than a band because the thread is almost invisible, the greatest care must be taken not to prick the horse with the needle or drop it in the bedding where it will almost certainly be lost and cause an injury at a later date.

How to plait a tail

A tidy tail shows off the horse's quarters and finishes a smart turnout. In order to plait a tail the hair must have been left to grow long on the dock, that is it should not have been pulled. Brush the tail through thoroughly before you start.

1. Take two small sections of hair from the very top left and top right of the tail.

2. Cross the right section diagonally over the left section, and hold with your left thumb and forefinger. Take another section from the right, just below the first so you now have three strands with which to plait.

3. Take another section from the left, adding it to the first, and fold them into the middle. Proceed downward in this way.

4. Keep taking sections from the left and right as you work down the tail, keeping the plait taut.

5. Decide where to finish the French plait, usually at the end of the hairless underneath part of the dock. Continue one long plait with just the hairs you are holding.

6. Put a band on the end to keep the plait in.

7. Fold the end of the single plait back up making a loop and secure with a band.

8. Tuck in any stray hairs or lay them flat with gel. Spray the plait with hairspray to help fix it in place. The tail will fan out better if the bottom is cut square.

Remember: Practice makes perfect, so work on it in your spare time!

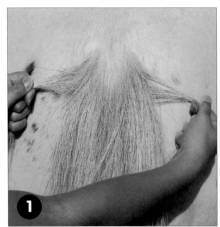

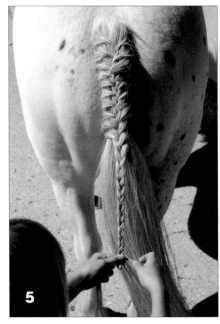

TIP Hair is easier to plait if it is not too clean and slippery. Wash it a couple of days before an event, and do not spray detangler on the dock section.

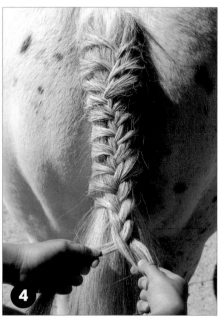

▲ **A well-plaited tail** *emphasizes the muscles of the horse's quarters.*

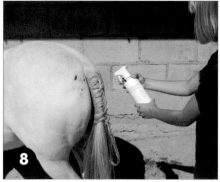

▶ **A natural tail** *will protect the horse more and takes very little upkeep because it can be plaited on the day of a show. A pulled tail looks tidy, but must be regularly thinned or pulled or it will resemble a bathroom brush!*

Putting on a tail bandage

Using a tail bandage will:
- Protect the tail from rubbing on the trailer should your horse be forced to lean back to keep his balance while the vehicle is moving.
- Keep the tail clean.
- Keep the hairs lying flat on a pulled tail and keep a plaited tail secure.

1. Hold the rolled-up bandage in one hand and pass the loose end under the dock and over the top of the tail as high up as possible.
2. Pass the rolled-up end across, fold the loose end downward, and then wind the bandage around again to hold the flap in place.
3. Work your way down the tail, winding the bandage in a diagonal downward direction.
4. Overlap the previous layer by half the width of the bandage each time.
5. Keep the bandage totally flat; any creases will dig in and be uncomfortable.
6. When you get to the end of the dock, change direction and go back upward, aiming to finish half way up.
7. Tie up using the tapes, looping them around, and tying on one side of the tail (to avoid a pressure spot if the horse leans on his tail).
8. You may find your horse now has an oddly shaped tail. Don't worry—just gently bend it into its natural curve.

TIP: If your horse has a light-colored tail, try using a long "bag" to contain the length of the tail, which can be held in place by the bandage overlapping it.

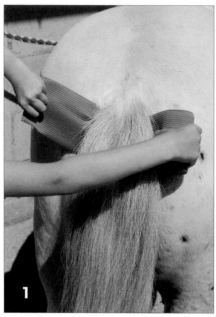

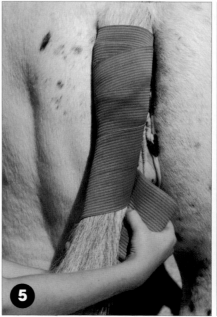

Remember: If you have bandaged over a plaited tail, unravel it gently so as not to disturb the hairs. With a natural or pulled tail, the best way to remove the bandage is to simply undo the tapes, hold the top of the bandage with both hands, and slide it all the way off. Keep your bandage tidy by rolling it up afterwards.

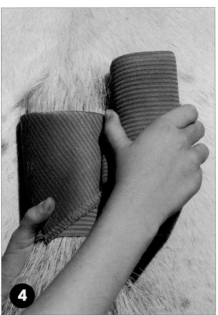

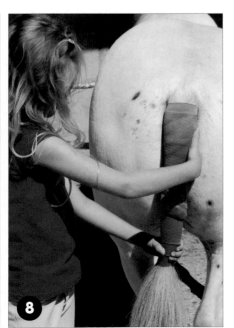

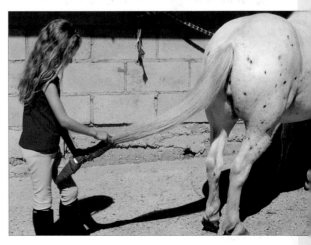

▲ **Undo tapes** *and slide down the bandage.*

Get ready to travel

Now that your horse is clean and tidy, you need to be able to transport him safely to show him off at a competition. Unfortunately, many horses are not keen on being transported due to fear caused by a previous bad experience, or just the feeling of unfamiliarity leaving companions and the claustrophobic environment inside the trailer.

The day of the show is not the time to be attempting to load our horse trailer for the first time, so start practicing beforehand.

Before the event:

1. If possible, leave the trailer somewhere in the yard where it can become a familiar feature to your horse.
2. Leave the ramp down (a trailer must be attached to a car for it to balance safely), and lead your horse up to it allowing him to sniff it.
3. Move any partitions to make the area seem as large possible.
4. By placing a bowl of feed inside, you may find his stomach will overrule any feelings of fear and he will march up the ramp willingly.
5. If he hesitates, do not rush him but reward any positive steps he takes with a treat or a stroke.
6. Ask someone to lead a well-behaved horse into the trailer first to give him confidence.
7. Once inside, give him some food and just stand there for a few minutes before leading him out again.
8. Practice regularly, feeding and grooming him inside the trailer so he is happy to be tied up in it.
9. Ask someone to put the ramp up while you watch

him, ideally with another horse beside him for added reassurance.
10. If possible, get him driven around on a short circular journey so he gets used to the motion but soon comes back to the security of his home.
GOAL: Practice so that your horse walks straight into the trailer the first time.

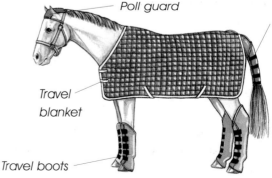

Poll guard

Tail bandage with tail guard

Travel blanket

Travel boots

TIP Learn the dress code for your particular class or event – looking good will give you added confidence.

GOING SHOWING – YOUR ACTION PLAN

Everyone is nervous when they first go to compete at a show. Will you remember all your equipment? How will your horse behave? How will you feel in the ring? What do you actually do when you get there to make sure you're entered in the right event? This checklist will help to calm your nerves by providing useful tips to help you prepare for the big day.

- Tell you instructor that your aim is to do a ridden show class
- Watch a show, or groom for a friend who is competing so you know the procedure— where to get your number, find the warmup arena, and the judging ring.
- Watch a video on showing and turnout so you can see what the judge will be looking for.
- Design your individual show. Keep it short and simple (walk, trot, and canter on both reins).
- Practice the halt and salute so your horse knows when to stand still.
- Pull or shorten your horse's mane if it is to be plaited; this may take a few sessions.
- Check that you have a showing jacket, shirt, and tie, and smart gloves and boots. You can buy good second-hand gear if you need to keep costs down.
- Practice bandaging your horse's legs, as well as loading him into a trailer. It is no good if you both looking perfect but you can't get to the show.

- Get schedules for local shows. These are often advertised in the local newspaper or pinned up in tack/feed shops.
- Ask friends to stand in line with you on their horses, and then watch you practice your individual display so that you won't be so nervous on show day.
- Send off your entry in plenty of time.
- Write a list of all the equipment you will need on the day of the event: clothing, tack, cleaning sprays, etc. And don't forget plenty of food and drink and a hay net for your horse!
- Bathe your horse a day or two before the show, and trim up any unruly hairs.
- Plait up on the morning of the show, and remove any stains on the coat. Cover your horse with a light travel blanket and put on his boots for the journey.
- Off you go, and good luck!

TREATING COMMON AILMENTS

Horse watching is one of the most informative ways of learning about horses. Watching natural behavior and being familiar with your horse's appearance and disposition on a daily basis should help to alert you if he is under the weather. Any changes to the way he looks or behaves may be indications that there are underlying health problems.

GET TO KNOW THE FACTS

- Find out, if possible, your horse's past medical history – if he is predisposed to certain ailments (such as laminitis) or has sustained any injury to a leg, for example, which might flare up at a later date.
- Be familiar with his habits. Does he eat his food readily? What is the normal consistency of his droppings, and how many piles a day? Does he lie down during the day or commonly rest a hind leg when standing?

- A horse's mucous membranes (the tissues behind the eyelids around the eyes and the gums in the mouth) should be salmon pink in color. If they are very white, this may indicate anemia (a condition caused by a lack of red blood cells that leads to feelings of tiredness). A yellow tinge could signify liver damage, perhaps due to poisoning.

▶ **Pulse/Heart Rate:** At rest a horse's heart rate should be between 30 and 40 beats per minute. It can be taken by pressing a finger on any artery, but is commonly taken under the horse's jaw.

◀ **Temperature:** The normal temperature of a horse is 100°F (38°C). A horse's temperature is usually taken by inserting the end of a thermometer about 1.75 in (4 cm) inside the rectum and holding it against the side of the bowel wall for about a minute.

◀ **Respiration:** The number of breaths a horse takes per minute should be between eight and twelve in a resting horse, but will increase after exercise. You can count the breaths by watching the sides of the horse expand and fall as the diaphragm moves.

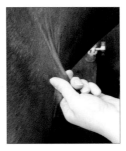

◀ **Hydration:** In a healthy horse, if you pinch the skin of the neck or shoulder between your fingers then release it, it should spring back flat quickly. If it is slow to flatten, this may be a sign of dehydration meaning that your horse has been deprived of water somehow.

▲ **A horse's pulse** *can be felt by locating the artery under the jaw, in the fetlock joint or in the girth area.*

TIP Keep a diary of the date and type of ailment – perhaps your mare is moody every three weeks when she is in season. It will help you to foresee problems.

HEALTH CHECK BEFORE RIDING

Is he alert, attentive, and pleased to see you?

Is there any discharge from his muzzle, or does he have dull, weepy eyes?

Are his eyes bright and clear?

Does he seem sullen and disinterested or bad-tempered toward you?

Are the mucous membranes around his eyes, nostrils, and gums a salmon-pink color?

Does he seem agitated, uncomfortable, or distressed?

Does his posture indicate he is sound?

Is he shifting his weight, resting his legs, head-shaking, or generally looking unsettled or uncomfortable?

 Do not think of riding until you have investigated the cause of the problem

 He appears to be healthy and happy, so continue

- **Check body visually.** Check the body and limbs for cuts, puncture wounds, bites, sores, girth galls, overreach grazes, mud fever, etc. Check that the legs are not puffy or swollen. Pick out hooves and check for excessive heat in them.
- **Check tack.** Check the fit of all tack and its positioning. Make sure all surfaces in contact with the skin are free of grease and mud, which could cause chafing.
- **Tighten girth straps gradually and check bit.** Check positioning of the bit in the mouth. Does the horse seem comfortable with it, or could there be a problem? Check for sores or cuts in the mouth.
- **Flex the horse before mounting.** Stretch out forelegs to eliminate pinching from the girth. Lead the horse in a small circle, to the left and to the right, to allow him to feel the tack and loosen up.
- **Mount slowly.** Ideally, mount from a mounting block and lower your weight gently into the saddle.
- **Warm up slowly.** Begin riding at a walk for a minimum of five minutes. Start on a loose rein to allow your horse to stretch out. He should be happy and interested in his work.

Recognizing & treating common ailments

Call your vet immediately if there is:
- Heavy bleeding
- Severe pain (obvious signs of distress include groaning, violent rolling, eyes rolling, straining)
- Sudden lameness or inability to move willingly
- A foreign body puncturing or embedded in the skin, such as a piece of wire
- Breathing difficulty
- Joint oil (a yellowish fluid) leaking from the wound
- An exposed bone

Keep a close eye on your horse, and arrange for the vet to visit as soon as possible if there is:
- A cut or puncture wound that has not caused lameness but may require flushing out or stitching
- Lameness, although the horse is able to walk
- Diarrhea or loss of appetite
- Mild colic (although this may pass before the vet arrives)
- Abnormal behavior, staggering or moving awkwardly, unusual aggression, or hypersensitive behavior
- Lumps or swellings or foul-smelling areas
- Recurrent coughing or discharge from the nose

COLIC

Colic is a general term to describe stomach pain. It could be caused by a buildup of gas, worm damage or compaction of food somewhere in the intestine causing a blockage, or a twist or dislodgement of part of the intestine. In severe cases, the horse will require emergency surgery for any chance of survival.

The symptoms of a horse or pony with colic are that he will appear uncomfortable – he may turn around and nudge or kick at his tummy, repeatedly try to roll, and grunt or groan. If he is suffering from eating too much or too quickly, it may be possible to walk the animal around to try to get the stomach and digestive system moving and allow the pain to subside. In all but the mildest cases, a vet should be called immediately because he may need to administer a drench (medicine given in liquid form) or muscle relaxants, or may need to refer the horse to a hospital for surgery.

LAMINITIS/FOUNDER

This is unfortunately a **very** common problem with horses. The laminae are sensitive tissues inside the hoof wall that cover the pedal bone. Any inflammation here will cause great pain, especially if the pedal bone has rotated too. In severe cases, it can even push through the sole of the foot. A laminitic horse will look in a sorry state as he tries to alleviate the pain in his feet by leaning back in an attempt to take the weight off the toes of the hoof. Both front feet and hind feet can be affected, but usually it is confined to the front feet.

In the wild, horses have to walk many miles each day in search of food, but when they live with us, they usually enjoy a more pampered domestic lifestyle with much less exercise and plentiful good grazing/hard feed simply given to them. This can often cause an

(TIP) If your horse's legs are painful with mud fever, there are herbal remedies that can be fed to help them heal without you needing to touch them.

▶ **The pain from** *a lame front leg can cause a horse to lift his head when walking as he tries to ease his weight off the bad leg.*

▶ **By contrast,** *a horse may lower his head if he is feeling pain in the hind leg as he transfers weight onto his front legs.*

▶ **Horses with laminitis** *stand with their weight on the heels of the affected hooves to relieve the pain experienced in the front of the hoof.*

▶ **A tired horse** *is more prone to injury, and a damaged ligament can mean months off work.*

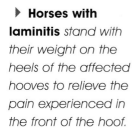

▶▶ **Applying petroleum jelly** *to dry, clean legs will act as a preventative barrier against mud fever.*

imbalance, triggering an attack. Working a horse on hard ground can also be a cause. However, too much rich grass is far and away the most common culprit.

If you suspect laminitis, call the vet immediately and in the meantime remove your horse from pasture and put him in a stable with a nice thick bed (shavings are best—they help to support the soles of the feet).

MUD FEVER

If you notice hard, crusty lumps of hair or scabs around the pasterns and heels of your horse, then it is likely he has mud fever. It is not actually a fever but a bacterial infection. It mainly occurs if horses are left in muddy conditions in which bacteria thrive.

When your horse is clean and dry, before he goes out in the field, protect his heels with a layer of petroleum jelly to act as a waterproofing barrier against the mud. If he does get plastered in mud, hose him off and dry his legs with a towel before putting him away. There are also "turnout socks" on the market that act like rubber boots for your horse.

The scabs will be hard and sore, but once a week put a hot, wet wrap around the pastern and leave it in place for five minutes. The warmth will help the scabs to soften, and you may be able to wipe some of them away. Dispose of all the cloths and scabs carefully so

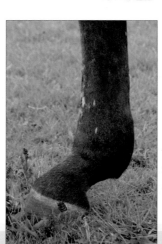

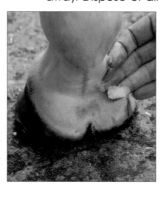

the bacteria does not spread. Treatment is made easier if the animal is also treated by adding herbal supplements to the feed designed to support the body in fighting the bacteria.

Recognizing & treating common ailments

THRUSH

If you pick out your horse's hoof and are faced with a foul smell and possible discharge, or if the frog appears to have loose edges (sometimes tinged grey or black), then he probably has an infection of the hoof called thrush. This is often caused by a horse standing for long

periods in wet conditions or in wet bedding, or if mud has not being picked out of the hoof regularly.

You will need to treat the area with an antiseptic spray and call your farrier who should trim back the frog to healthy tissue.

RAIN SCALD

This has similar symptoms to those of mud fever, but it is found predominantly along the length of the horse's back. Clumps of hair fall out and scabs may form when infection has taken hold. The cause is simply lack of protection from the elements, and it is usually caused by prolonged periods of rain saturating the horse's coat.

Thoroughly wash the horse with an antibacterial shampoo, feed a supplement to improve hair and skin condition, and use a blanket on the horse in wet weather. Nowadays there are different thicknesses of blankets available on the market so it is possible just to provide a rain sheet in milder conditions without risking the horse becoming overheated.

LICE AND MITES

If you notice your horse itching and scratching his neck, mane, or even the feathers on his legs, it is worth investigating to see if he has an infestation of lice or mites. These creatures are especially attracted to thick coats, and a particularly scurfy coat is often a sign of a problem. Horses rub these itchy areas, which can cause

bald patches and a tattered looking mane. There are powders and lotions that can be applied to kill the infestation or application of a flea treatment as prescribed for dogs can also be a very effective cure.

SWEET ITCH

Some animals are particularly sensitive to biting flies and midges and suffer an allergic reaction to the saliva of the biting flies. The result is that the areas (mainly the mane and tail) are extremely itchy and the horse tries to relieve the itch by rubbing and scratching the areas, causing bald patches and broken mane and tail hairs.

Soothing lotions can be applied to counter the itch/scratch cycle, but prevention is better than cure – and manes and tails take many months to grow! In warm weather (and particularly if your horse is kept near a stream or other water course where midges thrive), spray your horse with fly repellent, twice a day if

▲ **Constant scratching** *could be a sign of mites.*
▶ **Breathing problems** *can be caused by dust.*

Once the horse has contracted COPD, he will have to be kept away from anything that could irritate and inflame the breathing passages. Affected horses benefit from being turned out on grass. If kept inside, careful management is essential to ensure the provision of dust-free bedding. Feed only soaked hay to minimize the transmission of dust, molds, and spores that are often found in hay and straw.

necessary. Sponge down or hose him off if he is hot after a ride because a sweaty horse will attract midges like bees to honey, then reapply more fly repellent.

COUGHS/COPD

Some horses and ponies are more sensitive to contaminants in the air than others and can suffer from breathing problems. Bedding and hay often contain particles of dust, spores, and mold, which can trigger a repetitive cough or escalate into a form of asthma called COPD (chronic obstructive pulmonary disease). The lungs can become damaged and the poor animal has great difficulty breathing deeply enough to get adequate oxygen. You can sometimes see a "heave line" where the horse has strained to breathe.

Horrendous Hooves
Hooves are healthiest when their moisture content is kept more or less constant. Brittle hooves can be caused by the sudden change from a wet field to a dry bed of shavings.

First aid

If you own or care for a horse, a well-stocked first aid kit is essential. You never know when you might need to attend to some injury or illness, and it's sensible to have the basic remedies and materials on hand. Remember also to take first aid supplies in the trailer when you go to a show.

Your first aid kit should contain:

Thermometer 1: For checking the horse's temperature.

Dressings/gauze pads 2: To cover and protect wounds without sticking.

Gamgee padding 3: Used between dressings and bandages for support without causing pressure points.

Poultice pads 4: Can be cut to size and soaked in hot water to help treat hoof abscesses.

Roll of cotton wool 5: Used wet for cleaning wounds or as a bandage padding (not suitable as a dressing direct on a wound as fibers tend to stick to the wound).

Crepe elastic bandage 6: For use over padding for support and protection. Modern bandages stick to themselves for easy application.

Antibiotic spray 7: Helps prevent infection, and you can apply a spray without needing to touch the wound.

Scissors 8: For cutting dressings to size (use ones with rounded ends).

Adhesive tape 9: For holding dressings and poultices in place.

Iodine/salt 10: Either can be added to water to make a solution for flushing wounds clean.

Wound powder 11: Prevents infection from entering a wound; useful on a small nick that cannot be bandaged. Do not use if you have called the vet because it will hinder his examination.

Tweezers 12: To remove splinters, thorns etc.

Petroleum jelly 13: To protect areas prone to chafing (e.g., girth galls) and to lubricate the thermometer before it is inserted.

Disposable gloves 14: Useful when applying ointments and to prevent infection passing from your hands into a wound.

Have a notice or blackboard clearly visible in the yard or tackroom that displays helpful telephone numbers, including those of your vet and farrier, just in case someone needs to contact them urgently in your absence.

HOW TO DEAL WITH MINOR INJURIES

It is best to practice bandaging a leg while your horse is uninjured – both you and he will be calm and you can develop your skills in a stress-free situation. Then, if he does get a cut, you will feel more confident that you will be able to cope. Remember, if you have any doubts about the severity of the wound, call your vet. Only bandage small wounds that are not near any joints; otherwise seek professional advice.

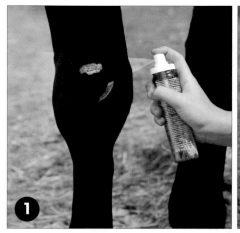

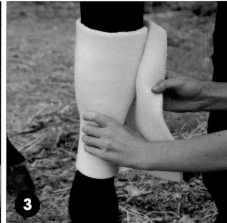

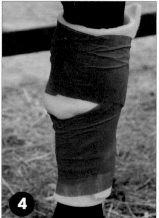

Remember: Never use cotton as a dressing directly onto the wound or the fibers will stick to it. Cotton can be used to clean the wound provided it is wet or positioned behind a dressing as padding.

HOW TO BANDAGE A LEG WOUND

1. Flush out the wound with saline or iodine solution or a wound wash. Apply a healing antiseptic wound gel (omit this if the vet is coming to examine the horse).
2. Cover the wound with a nonstick dressing pad.
3. Use a large piece of absorbent wadding or gamgee (absorbent cushioned padding for leg support and protection) behind it to absorb any discharge and to help support the limb and reduce swelling.
4. Apply a stretch bandage to hold everything in place. This can either be cohesive, which will stick to itself, or a cotton bandage tied around the limb and then secured with tape. Leave a gap in the bandage to allow the joint to flex.
5. Bandage the opposite leg just with gamgee and an elastic bandage to help support it -- your horse will put more weight on it to avoid using the injured leg.

Index

Note: Page numbers set in *italic type* refer to captions; page numbers set in **bold type** indicate the main subject reference.

Index and Picture Credits

Picture Credits

Unless otherwise credited below, all the photographs in this book were taken by **Neil Sutherland** especially for Interpet Publishing.

iStockphoto.com:
Hugh Alison: 3 bottom right, 32 top right.
Jeffrey Banke: 11 top inset.
Nicholas Belton: 40 left.
Mark Bond: 50 center.
Neil Bradfield: 58 bottom right, 85.
Deborah Calnan: 55 top right.
Phil Cardamone: 76 left.
Roberta Casaliggi: 16 left.
Deborah Cheramie: 25 bottom left, 77 top left.
Cathleen Clapper: 81 top right.
Barry Crossley: 6 top right, 8 bottom right, 11 bottom inset, 35 bottom right, 59, 64, 69 top center, 75 top, 84 center right.
Jody Dingle: 52 bottom right.
Philip Downs: 84 bottom left.
Carol Gering: 1.
Hedda Gjerpen: Front cover (main image), 2, 3 top right, 29 bottom left, 29 bottom right, 46 top right, 74 bottom.
Tim Goff: 90 top right.
Anja Hild: 17 bottom left.
Loretta Hostettler: 18 center left.
Rick Hyman: 33 bottom right.
Melissa Jones: 25 top left, 57 bottom center.
Joseph C. Justice: 27 top left.
Julia Kappus: 86 inset of muzzle.
Ann Kitzman: 6 bottom right.
Mikhail Kondrashov: 77 bottom right.
Konstantin32: 10 inset.
Geoff Kuchera: 7 bottom right.

Markanja: 9 pie chart, 26 top left.
Julie Masson: 3 left.
Kary Nieuwenhuis: 12 top right, 29 top.
Tamir Niv: 8 top right.
Pedro Nogueira: 56 carrots.
Angela Oakes: 53 center right, 58 bottom left.
Simon Owler: 25 bottom center.
Grant Shimmin: 20 top right.
Eline Spek: 7 top left.
Baldur Tryggvason: 9 top right, 39 center left, 39 bottom left, 51 top center, 53 top left.
Neil Walton: 17 bottom right.
Zastavkin: 72 left.
Jeanette Zehentmayer: 12 center right.

Shutterstock.com:
Catnap: 14-15 bottom.
Electerra: 91 top left.
Judy ben Joud: 26 bottom right.
Ryan Klos: 91 center right.
Mikhail Evgenevich Kondrashov: 24 center left.
Abramova Kseniya: 8 bottom left.
Kathryn Rapier: 41 top right.
Scott Sanders: 14-15 top, 16 bottom right.
Otmar Smit: 7 bottom left.

Published by
Interpet Publishing,
Vincent Lane,
Dorking,
Surrey RH4 3YX,
England
Editor: Philip de Ste. Croix
Designer: Philip Clucas MCDS
Photographer: Neil Sutherland
Diagram artwork: Maggie Raynor
Index: Amanda O'Neill
Production management:
Consortium, Suffolk
Print production: Sino Publishing House Ltd, Hong Kong

Disclaimer

Warning
Riding is a hazardous pastime. Horses are unpredictable, powerful animals and even something as simple as leading a horse in from a field can potentially be dangerous. Never underestimate the situation and think ahead. It is advisable to carry a mobile phone and always wear a hard hat and protective clothing when riding. Seek help if you are unsure about any aspect of horsecare or equitation.